Spotlight On

Paris

Carole French

Written by Carole French

Published by AA Publishing, a trading name of Automobile Association Developments Limited, whose registered office is Fanum House, Basing View, Basingstoke, Hampshire, RG21 4EA. Registered number 1878835.

Packaged for Automobile Association Developments Limited by IL&FS, New Delhi

A CIP catalogue record for this book is available from the British Library.

ISBN 978-0-7495-5475-0

The contents of this publication are believed correct at the time of printing. Nevertheless, the publishers cannot be held responsible for any errors or omissions or for changes in the details given in this guide or for the consequences of any reliance on the information provided by the same. Assessments of attractions, hotels, restaurants and so forth are based on the author's own experience and, therefore, descriptions given in this guide necessarily contain an element of subjective opinion which may not reflect the publishers' opinion or dictate a reader's own experience on another occasion. We have tried to ensure accuracy in this guide, but things do change and we would be grateful if readers would advise us of any inaccuracies they may encounter.

Colour separation by KDP
Printed and bound in China by Leo Paper Products

A03233
Maps in this title produced from map data © Tele Atlas N.V. 2006
Transport map © Communicarta Ltd, UK

CONTENTS

Around the Tour Eiffel

Latin Quarter, St-Germain & Islands

Marais and Bastille

ouvre and Champs-lysées

Montmartre

Further Afield

PARIS

With a history spanning centuries, fabulous architecture from the medieval and baroque periods to the modern day, and a multicultural society that offers art, music and theatre, endless sporting opportunities and high cuisine, Paris beckons all. For the 2 million-plus residents it offers a great lifestyle, but even if you are visiting for a weekend, it can be magical. For those who simply want to relax and absorb the atmosphere for a few days, enjoy the public parks, shop for designer fashions or study the architecture, Paris will not fail to enchant you.

The thoroughly multicultural, cosmopolitan city of today is a far cry from the Paris of centuries past, when it started life as a tiny community nestling on what is now the Île de la Cité. One of the greatest cities in the world, it is a place that everyone should visit at least once in their lifetime. If you can, you should return to the city time and again to experience it at different times of the year. Each season has its own special charm in Paris.

Springtime brings the locals out in droves, sipping coffee at pavement cafés, jogging or taking a stroll in the great parks, such as the Jardin du Luxembourg or the Jardin des Tuileries, both a hive of activity on a Sunday morning. Summer, when most Parisians head for holiday homes by the sea, brings out-of-town visitors keen to see the sights, while in autumn the parks turn a subtle shade of gold, and winter brings frosty mornings and Christmas in this magical city. The Champs-Élysées dressed in white festive lights in winter is a stunning sight that will remain in the memory long after the visit.

The visitor to Paris today will find glorious ecclesiastical buildings from the great Notre-Dame, seat of the Archbishop of Paris that has stood on the Île de la Cité since the 14th century, to the even earlier but little known Romanesque-style Église Saint-Germain-des-Prés, which dates back to the 10th century. The latter is located

Rodin and Pablo Picasso in the Musée Picasso, and the contemporary exhibits housed in the Musée d'Orsay on the Left Bank, or in the overtly modern, brightly coloured Centre Georges Pompidou.

Further afield, the mighty Château de Versailles, former home of royalty, or Chantilly, with its outstanding reputation for horse racing, are absolute musts on the sightseeing agenda.

Paris is not a museum, however. It is an exuberant place where residents and visitors alike enjoy life to the full. There are art galleries that stay open all night during special annual events, and restaurants offering food from all corners of the world, including Oriental, Mexican, Italian and Indian, in addition, of course, to the finest French cuisine.

There are numerous cultural events and festivities to enjoy in Paris, such as the great Fête de la Musique, during which Parisians and visitors of all ages party on the streets. Then, of course, there are the world's greatest fashion houses. Head for the rue du Faubourg Saint-Honoré, not far from the Ópera Palais Garnier, to endulge in major designer names such as Versace, Gucci, Karl Lagerfield and Hermés to name just a few.

Add to this walks in the great parks, Sunday mornings in marketplaces full of animated conversation, watching street performers or taking one of the bateaux for a leisurely trip along the Seine and you will discover why the city is so special.

Most visitors come to Paris to see its world renowned historic landmark buildings, which have survived revolutions, attacks and wars, to see stunning modern architecture, or simply to enjoy the lively atmosphere, if only for a weekend.

No matter how many times you visit, the city never ceases to inspire. Romantic, historic, theatrical, artistic, architecturally fascinating, an art lover's dream, and a gourmet's delight – Paris has something for everyone.

amid the vibrant hustle and bustle of the busy Left Bank.

The main sites that everyone who visits Paris will want to see are, without doubt: the Tour Eiffel standing proud and serene watching over the city; Les Invalides, site of the tomb of Napoleon I; the neo-Romanesque-Byzantine Sacré-Coeur, on the hill at Montmartre; the Musée du Louvre, home to over 35,000 priceless works of art; the Arc de Triomphe, which is directly in the line of sight from the Musée du Louvre; the Place de la Concorde; and the futuristic La Grande Arche at La Défense on the outskirts of the city.

Museum enthusiasts will be enthralled by the works of Auguste Rodin in the Musée

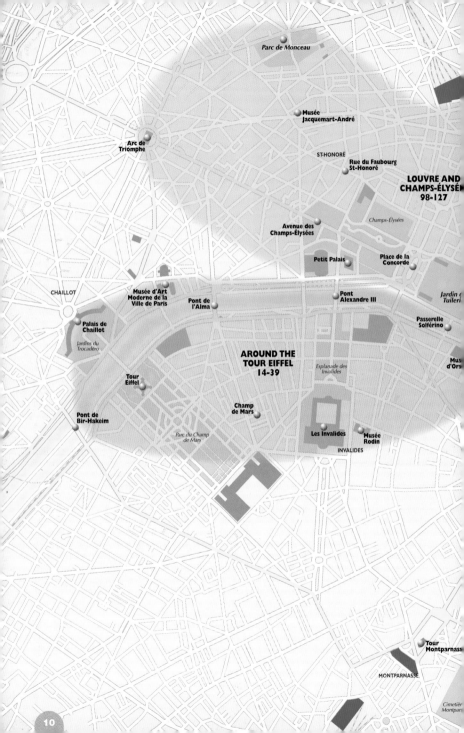

Parc de Monceau

Musée
Jacquemart-André

Arc de
Triomphe

ST-HONORÉ

Rue du Faubourg
St-Honoré

**LOUVRE AND
CHAMPS-ÉLYSÉ
98-127**

Champs-Élysées

Avenue des
Champs-Élysées

Place de la
Concorde

Petit Palais

CHAILLOT

Musée d'Art
Moderne de la
Ville de Paris

Pont de
l'Alma

Pont
Alexandre III

Jardin
Tuileri

Palais de
Chaillot

Passerelle
Solférino

Jardins du
Trocadéro

**AROUND THE
TOUR EIFFEL
14-39**

Esplanade des
Invalides

Mus
d'Ors

Tour
Eiffel

Champ
de Mars

Pont de
Bir-Hakeim

Parc du Champ
de Mars

Les Invalides

Musée
Rodin

INVALIDES

Tour
Montparnass

MONTPARNASSE

Cimetièr
Montpar

10

GUIDE TO BOOK REGIONS

0   500 m

0   500 yds

Musée
Gustave
Moreau

Printemps &
Jeries Lafayette

Drouot
Richelieu

Opéra
Palais
Garnier

Galerie
Colbert

Galerie
Vivienne

Musée
des Arts
et Métiers

Jardin du
Palais Royal

St-
Eustache

LES HALLES

Jardin du Forum
des Halles

Musée d'Art
et d'Histoire
du Judaïsme

Musée du
Louvre

Centre Georges
Pompidou

Café
Beaubourg

Rue Vieille-
du-Temple

Musée
Picasso

Pont
Royal

St-Merri

**MARAIS AND
BASTILLE
76-97**

Musée
Cognacq-Jay

Seine

Pont
des Arts

Pont
Neuf

LE
MARAIS

Musée
Carnavalet

Square du
Vert-Galant

Seine

Rue des
Rosiers

Rue Jacob

ConcIergerie

ST-GERMAIN-
DES-PRÉS

Maison Européenne
de la Photographie

Place des
Vosges

St-
Germain-
des-Prés

Sainte-
Chapelle

Île de
la Cité

BASTILLE

Café de Flore &
es Deux Magots

Mariage
Frères

La Seine

Rue du
Cherche-
Midi

St-Sulpice

Notre-
Dame

Pont
Marie

Île St-Louis

Pavillon de
l'Arsenal

Musée de
Cluny

St-Séverin

Mémorial
des Martyrs de la
Déportation

**LATIN QUARTER,
ST-GERMAIN AND
ISLANDS
40-75**

La Sorbonne

QUARTIER
LATIN

Institut
du Monde
Arabe

St-Étienne-
du-Mont

Jardin du
Luxembourg

Arènes
de Lutèce

Rue Vavin

Jardin des
Plantes

Musée National
d'Histoire Naturelle

Bibliothèque
Nationale de France-
François Mitterrand

Around the Tour Eiffel

With the Tour Eiffel dominating the scene and the dramatic semicircular Palais de Chaillot and its fountains on one side, the gold dome of Les Invalides glistening on the other, and a glimpse of the Pont Alexandre III along the River Seine, you have an area of Paris that is extraordinarily beautiful. Visit the museums, take a boat ride, relax in the Champ de Mars park, or simply sit and admire the impressive architecture. By night, the buildings are subtly illuminated, changing the atmosphere yet again for both visitors and the well-heeled residents who are lucky enough to have their homes here.

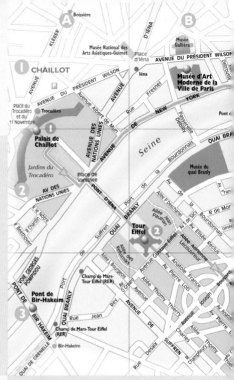

AROUND THE TOUR EIFFEL WALK

1. Place du Trocadéro and Palais de Chaillot
See page 28

Place du Trocadéro is surrounded by traditional Parisian architecture, but it is the Palais de Chaillot and the view of the Tour Eiffel across its central terrace that dominates the skyline. Take the route down a series of steps, past the fountains in the Jardins du Trocadéro. Cross over at the Place de Varsovie and walk across the Pont d'Iéna to the Tour Eiffel.

2. Tour Eiffel
See page 34

The most famous of all the landmarks in Paris, the Tour Eiffel is a must on any walker's agenda. Stand underneath for an unconventional view of the 324m (1,063 feet) high structure. Then walk through the Parc du Champ de Mars and across the Motte-Picquet, which takes you to the somewhat austere façade of the École Militaire.

3. École Militaire and Parc du Champ de Mars
See page 18

Most famous as the school where Napoleon Bonaparte trained as an officer in 1784, the École Militaire was founded in the mid-18th century by Louis XV. It faces the Parc du Champ de Mars, which was at one time used for training the French army. Now head eastwards along the avenue de Tourville and left into the boulevard de la Tour Maubourg, which leads you to the Les Invalides.

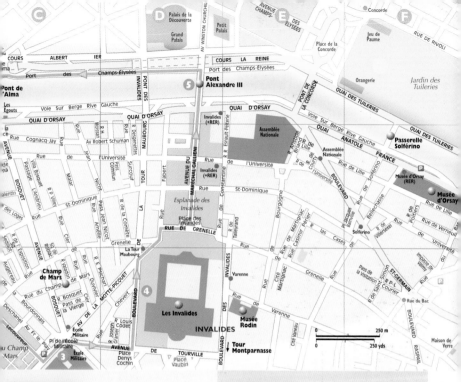

4. Les Invalides
See page 19

With a dome said to be covered in over 550,000 leaves of gold, Les Invalides (Hôtel des Invalides) is an imposing building that was formerly used as a charitable hospital for aged soldiers. It houses the tomb of Napoleon I and an army museum. From here take a stroll along the wide, open avenue du Maréchal Gallieni and across the Pont Alexandre III.

5. Pont Alexandre III
See page 30

Without doubt one of the prettiest and most elaborate of all the bridges that span the Seine, the art nouveau-style Pont Alexandre III was built between 1896 and 1900. Cherubs, horses and lamps make it an imposing sight. Look out for the Grand Palais and Petit Palais museum buildings ahead of you, and turn left to take a riverside walk back to the place de Varsovie, with the Palais de Chaillot to your right up the steps.

Champ de Mars

The large expanse of lawns at the Champ de Mars, dotted with colourful flowerbeds, provides the perfect setting to admire the view below the Tour Eiffel, all the way to the Palais de Chaillot and the fountains of the Jardins du Trocadéro.

On the opposite side of the tower, in sharp contrast, is the austere façade of the École Militaire, designed by Jacques-Ange Gabriel. Many young soldiers have entered its doors. Most famous among them was Napoleon Bonaparte. He completed his training in just one year instead of the required two, and in the late 1700s went on to change the course of European history.

The Champ de Mars was originally designed as an army training school and parade ground in 1765. However, it later went on to host horse races (the first in 1780) and to become the centre for numerous revolutionary celebrations.

It even saw Joseph-Michael and Jacques-Étienne Montgolfier, the inventors of the hot-air balloon, stage ballooning experiments on the lawns in the mid- to late 1700s. During the late 19th century it was used as a vast exhibition ground and venue for the 1889 World's Fair.

Today, this is a popular park for those who seek tranquillity in the bustling city – there is even a wall in the grounds with the word 'peace' written in 32 languages and 13 alphabets.

Above: A view of the verdant Champ de Mars from the Tour Eiffel

- 17 C3
- Champ de Mars
- www.monument-paris. com
- 24 hours
- Free
- École Militaire

Les Invalides

A wide, impressive façade, a glistening dome said to be covered with 550,000 leaves of gold and an extensive cobbled courtyard skirting huge triangular lawns make Les Invalides (or Hôtel des Invalides, as it is often called) an appropriate spot for the final resting place of one of France's greatest personalities.

Napoleon Bonaparte, one of the most prominent generals during the French Revolution, and Emperor of France for 10 years from 1804 (and again briefly in 1815) was laid to rest here. His body was brought to St Jerome's Chapel in Paris in 1840 following his death on St Helena. However, during an extensive renovation of Les Invalides a few years later in 1861, his tomb was positioned directly under the great dome in the royal chapel – the Église du Dôme. His grandiloquent sarcophagus is 'guarded' by 12 statues and includes coffins within coffins, made of wood, iron and lead.

Les Invalides was originally commissioned by Louis XIV in 1670 and designed by the architect Libéral Bruant as a military hospital and retirement home for war veterans. It was completed

Above: The façade of Les Invalides, which was formerly a home for wounded soldiers, and now houses an army museum

✚ **17 D3**

✉ **Les Invalides**
boulevard des Invalides

☎ 01 44 42 38 77

🌐 **www.invalides.org**

🕐 Daily summer 10–6; winter 10–5; closed public holidays and first Mon of month

✋ Moderate

🚇 RER Line C Invalides

Left: A cannon in the courtyard of Les Invalides. The building was commissioned to house retired soldiers
Above: The Église du Dôme des Invalides, built by Jules Hardouin-Mansart, viewed past a verdigris statue
Right: The dome of Les Invalides was added in 1708

in 1676, albeit without its famous dome and the chapel beneath it. These structures were commissioned a few years later, and Jules Hardouin Mansart, along with Bruant, drew up plans for the chapel, complete with baroque-style columns and cupolas. The dome, inspired by St Peter's Basilica in Rome, is widely recognised as one of the finest baroque architectural triumphs in France. Work on the chapel and dome was finished in 1708.

Externally, the vast 196m (643 feet) long classical façade and majestic Cour d'Honneur are stunning examples of architectural expertise. The latter is an open paved courtyard overlooked by carved

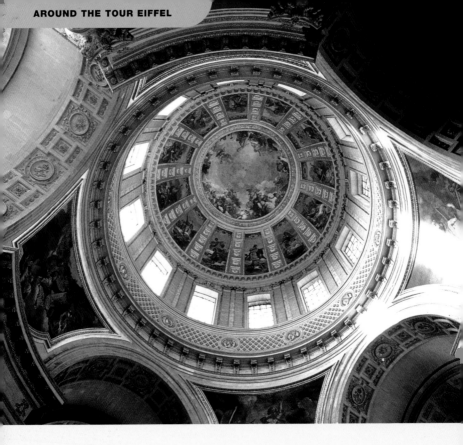

horses trampling the emblems of war in adjoining pavilions, while the gardens provide a restful interlude. On either side of the great courtyard lie the two wings of the Musée de l'Armée.

The best way to approach the building and to really appreciate its size and grandeur is from the Pont Alexandre III and along the avenue du Maréchal Gallieni.

Inside, along with Napoleon I's sarcophagus, are the tombs of other members of his family who were also leading military figures, as well as those of Turenne, Lyautey and Foch.

The Musée de l'Armée, dedicated to French military history from its early days to World War II, is also housed here.

François I's armour, various standards from different periods and a fascinating oriental collection, complete with a dragon mask for horses, are seen alongside the replica of the room where Napoleon died in exile on St Helena after his defeat at Waterloo. Notice Napoleon's campaign tent, clothing, hat and even his horse, Vizir, which has been stuffed for posterity.

A moving exhibition of photographs, film clips and artefacts tells the story of World War II. It occupies several floors in the south wing.

Above: A view from the floor up into the dome inside Les Invalides

Musée d'Art Moderne de la Ville de Paris

Strikingly modern in appearance, as befits its purpose, this extensive museum was built in 1937 and recently underwent large-scale renovations. It houses works by some of the world's finest 20th-century contemporary masters.

La Danse, a mural by Henri Matisse, and *La Ville de Paris*, by Robert Delaunay, along with Raoul Duffy's works are among the 'must sees' here. The collections feature *nouveau réalisme* and abstract, along with fauvism, cubism and surrealism. A combination of permanent exhibitions, including a room dedicated to works by Duffy, the most significant of which is the massive and beautifully presented *La Fée Électricité*, and regular temporary displays of the world's leading collections, make this museum a popular site.

Next to the museum, the Palais de Tokyo has an outstanding collection of modern works in its Centre d'Art Contemporain, and has pioneered the idea of museums staying open until midnight.

Above: Installations and other exhibits of contemporary art at the Musée d'Art Moderne

✚ **16 B1**

✉ **Musée d'Art Moderne de la Ville de Paris**
11 avenue du Président-Wilson

☎ 01 53 67 40 00

🌐 **www.mam.paris.fr**

🕐 Tue, Wed, Thu, Sun 10–6, Fri, Sat 10–8; closed Aug. Centre d'Art Contemporain Tue–Sun noon–midnight

✋ Moderate

🚇 Iéna, Alma-Marceau

Musée d'Orsay

Housed in one of the most extraordinary Victorian buildings on the Left Bank of the Seine, the Musée d'Orsay should not be overlooked even by those who are not art enthusiasts. This enormous structure, which was once the Orsay railway station, has received both acclaim and criticism following its renovation. It retains its steel infrastructure, giving it a contemporary feel, and large expanses of glass in its ceiling and walls make it luminous and airy. Works are displayed on massive, freestanding stone 'walls' that offer a sense of architectural equilibrium with the metal and glass.

A national museum, it displays prominent Western art collections ranging from 1848 to 1914, without favouring any one style. In fact, everything from fauvism and realism, to symbolism and naturalism is on display. It is truly an art lover's paradise, whatever you wish to see.

The ground floor, for instance, hosts an impressive collection of classic 19th-century paintings, combined with sculptures and *objets d'art*, while the upper levels have galleries displaying the works of Monet, Cézanne, Van Gogh, Renoir and Degas. Contemporary collections are housed in the mid-level areas, along with sculptures by Rodin and Emile-Antoine Bourdelle.

Guest collections from the Louvre and the Musée National d'Art Moderne are a regular feature. Try not to miss the Salle des Fêtes, a beautiful mirrored room with a massive chandelier, once part of the hotel in the railway station. It has been preserved as a reminder to the building's history.

Left: A view of the interior of the Musée d'Orsay, which was once a railway station
Above: A piece of classical sculpture at the museum

✚ **17 F2**

✉ **Musée d'Orsay**
62 rue de Lille

☎ 01 40 49 48 14

 www.musee-orsay.fr

🕓 Tue–Sun 9:30–6,
Thu 9:30am–9:45pm

✋ Moderate, first Sun of the month free

🚇 RER Line C Musée d'Orsay

Musée Rodin

Auguste Rodin, one of the world's greatest sculptors of the modern age, lived here from 1908 until his death in 1917. The rococo-style 18th-century mansion sits amid gardens of several hectares, and houses a relatively small museum that is an elegant tribute to a master. Uses as a dance hall, an artist's studio and a convent, it became a museum to Rodin's memory in 1919, and houses a remarkable collection of his works.

Among the exhibits are early sketches, which are fascinating in their detail, and a series of watercolour paintings and sepia photographs. But the works that make you stop in your tracks are his widely celebrated white marble and bronze statues. The greatest of these is *The Kiss*, quite beautiful in its simplicity. Other works include busts of the writer Victor Hugo and composer Mahler, along with those by Rodin's contemporaries, including Renoir, Monet, Van Gogh and his mistress and fellow artist Camille Claudel. More of Rodin's masterpieces, such as *Le Baiser* and *La Cathédrale,* can be found on the ground floor of the museum.

Great works, such as *The Thinker*, *The Burghers of Calais* bronze cast and *The Gates of Hell* can be seen in the extensive landscaped gardens, which are the third largest in Paris. They are open to the public and well worth a visit.

Left: A garden containing some of the exhibits of the Musée Rodin, in the grounds of Hôtel Biron, where Rodin lived from 1907 to his death in 1917
Above: An exhibit from the Musée Rodin

✠ **17 E3**

✉ **Musée Rodin**
Hôtel Biron, 79 rue de Varenne

☎ 01 44 18 61 10

www **www.musee-rodin.fr**

🕐 Tue–Sun Apr–Sep 9:30–5:45, Oct–Mar 9:30–4:45

✋ Moderate

🚇 Varenne

Palais de Chaillot

One spot in Paris never fails to attract photographers – whether professionals or amateurs – and this is the terrace between the two wings of the semicircular Palais de Chaillot. Superb views from here extend over the Jardins du Trocadéro, past the fountains and lake, and across the Seine to the Tour Eiffel.

The palace was purpose-built for the 1937 Exposition Universelle to an art deco-inspired design. Contemporary bronze statues are artistically placed between its elegant columns, enhancing the architecture.

The purpose of the building was to house a number of museums, as well as the Théâtre National de Chaillot, which at one time was the centre of cultural life in Paris. The most notable of the museums is the Musée de l'Homme, devoted to anthropology, and the Musée de la Marine,

one of the largest maritime museums in the world. It is part of a network of venues that include those in Brest, Rochefort, Toulon and Port-Louis. A wealth of exhibits is housed here; books, maps, blueprints and photographs, along with navigation

equipment, diving suits, weapons and replica ships. Some of the artefacts date back to the 17th century.

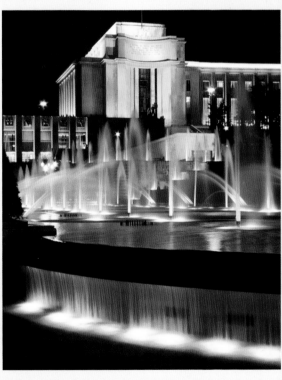

Below: Fountains glitter at night in the architectural complex of the Palais de Chaillot, designed for the 1937 world exhibition, and now home to major museums of the city

 16 A2

✉ **Palais de Chaillot**
   17 place du Trocadéro

☎ 01 53 65 69 69

🌐 **www.musee-marine.fr**

🕐 Daily Wed–Mon 10–6;
   closed some public
   holidays

✋ Moderate

🚇 Trocadéro

Passerelle Solférino

Paris is a city of contrasting architectural periods and innovative themes. This became evident with the unveiling of one its more recent landmarks – the Passerelle Solférino, a handsomely designed and crafted wooden arched footbridge that spans the Seine from the Musée d'Orsay on the Left Bank to the quayside next to the Jardins des Tuileries on the right.

Designed by architect Marc Mimram after an international competition was conducted to find a innovative design, the bridge opened in November 1999. It underwent exhaustive tests, including one that involved 150 people dancing in unison, to reveal any flaws in the design. Shortly after its official opening it swayed a couple of centimetres, which forced its closure for a day.

Nonetheless, the 106m (348-foot) long bridge has since been declared entirely safe, and hundreds of people cross from one side of the river to the other each day, stopping awhile to view the city from one of the benches along its length.

Above: A tunnel view across the covered Passerelle Solférino bridge

🕇 **17 F2**

✉ **Passerelle Solférino**
quai des Tuileries or quai Anatole

🕐 Daily

🎟 Free

Ⓜ Solférino

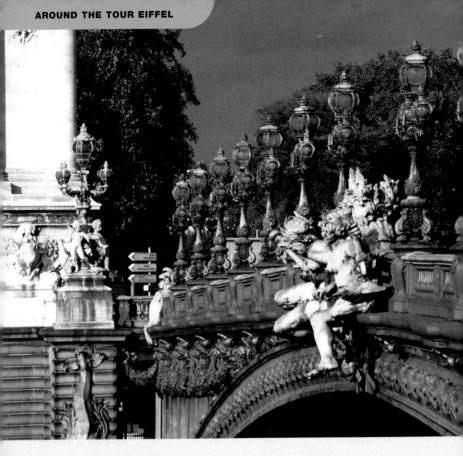

Pont Alexandre III

One of the landmarks of Paris and widely regarded as the most beautiful of all the bridges that span the Seine, the Pont Alexandre III links the Grand Palais and the Petit Palais on the Right Bank with Les Invalides on the Left Bank. It is aligned perfectly with the Esplanade des Invalides, giving an unobstructed view of the massive façade of the military building. It took three years to build, based on the designs of engineers Jean Résal and Amédée Alby, and was named after Tsar Alexander III.

Four gilded bronze-winged horses adorn columns at either end of the bridge, which is lavishly decorated with sculptures, nymphs and cherubs – the work of around 15 different artists. On either side of the road are lamp posts in an elaborate art nouveau style, while the overall design reflects the architecture of the Grand Palais.

Officially regarded as a historical monument, the bridge was unveiled for the first time in 1900 for the Exposition Universelle and has been a firm favourite with Parisians and visitors alike.

A 6m (18-foot) high steel arch spans the river, giving the bridge the distinction of being one of the finest examples of 19th-century engineering.

Above: The Pont Alexandre III is seen as an example of the optimism of the belle époque style
Above right: Allegorical sculptures adorn the Pont Alexandre III at either end of the bridge

✚ **17 D1**

✉ **Pont Alexandre III**
Cours de la Reine and Quai d'Orsay

☎ 24 hours

✋ Free

🚇 Invalides, Champs-Élysées, Clémenceau

Pont de l'Alma

The first Pont de l'Alma was built between 1854 and 1856 to commemorate the Franco-British victory over Russia in the Crimean War. It was unveiled by Napoleon III. The present bridge is the second structure built on the site. The first bridge was replaced in 1974 when it developed structural problems.

The present bridge has a statue of a Zouave (a member of the French military) that is used to measure the level of the Seine. When the water rises to the level of the statue's feet the roads on either side of the river generally close.

The Pont de l'Alma is at the beginning of the underpass where Diana, Princess of Wales, died in August 1997. The Liberty Flame, a symbol of American and French friendship, erected in 1987, has become an unofficial monument to Diana, and flowers are still laid here in her memory.

Right: The statue of a Zouave in the river is used to measure the water level

✚ **17 C1**

✉ **Pont de l'Alma**
place de l'Alma and place de la Résistance

🕐 24 hours

✋ Free

Ⓜ Alma-Marceau

Pont de Bir-Hakeim

Originally built for pedestrians in 1878, this bridge was given a new lease of life in 1905 when it was rebuilt to a dramatic two-tier art nouveau design. It comprises two metal parts on either side of the Allée des Cygnes, with a roadway, path and cycle track running along its length, and a metro viaduct above.

Connecting Passy on the Right Bank with Bir-Hakeim on the Left Bank, it became known as the Pont de Bir-Hakeim in 1949 in memory of the battle of Bir Hakeim and General Koenig's victory in Libya in 1942–3.

Elegant supporting columns make this an extremely graceful structure. A series of plaques in memory of fallen soldiers decorates the bridge, while four stone statues are located at the access point to the Islands of the Swans (Ile des Cygnes), a charming artificial island in the Seine.

Left: Pont de Bir-Hakeim's elegant supports place it among the most beautiful old bridges across the Seine

✚ **16 A3**

✉ **Pont de Bir-Hakeim**
   quai Branly and avenue du Président Kennedy

🕐 24 hours

💶 Free

Ⓜ Bir-Hakeim, Passy

Tour Eiffel

With more than 6.7 million visitors every year, the Tour Eiffel is possibly the most popular landmark in Paris. As you stand underneath and gaze at the enormous structure, or look across the Palais de Chaillot that passes below the tower to the Champ de Mars and the École Militaire on the other side, the Tour Eiffel's pre-eminence becomes evident.

The tower was built for the Exposition Universelle of 1889, and was considered by many to be an apt monument to celebrate the centenary of the French Revolution. Erected in an amazingly short time, the tower – the tallest structure in the world at that time – took just over two years to build, with 300 workers putting in long hours from January 1887 to March 1889. Over 5,000 drawings were created from the design of Gustave Eiffel, a widely respected and prolific builder of cast-iron structures, who

won a competition for the best design. His other works include churches, viaducts and bridges around the world.

The Tour Eiffel, one of his most challenging creations, was never intended to be a permanent structure. At the time, it drew widespread criticism, with many claiming that not only did it spoil the skyline of the city but was potentially unsafe. It was almost pulled down at one point, but by 1910 it had become so widely accepted and loved that it was given a new lease of life. Confirming Gustave's claims of safety,

Above: The Tour Eiffel seen from the top of the Tour Montparnasse

✚ **16 B2**

✉ **Tour Eiffel**
Champ de Mars

☎ 01 44 11 23 23

🔳 **www.tour-eiffel.fr**

🕐 Daily 9:30am–11pm; mid-Jun to beginning Sep 9am–midnight

✋ Expensive

🚇 Bir-Hakeim, Trocadéro

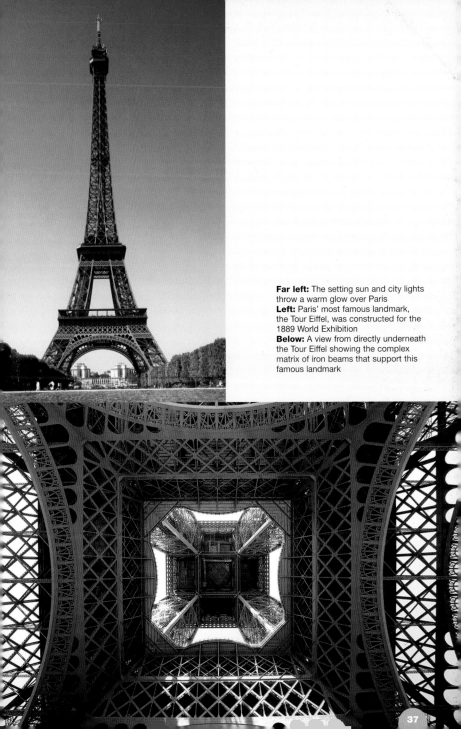

Far left: The setting sun and city lights throw a warm glow over Paris
Left: Paris' most famous landmark, the Tour Eiffel, was constructed for the 1889 World Exhibition
Below: A view from directly underneath the Tour Eiffel showing the complex matrix of iron beams that support this famous landmark

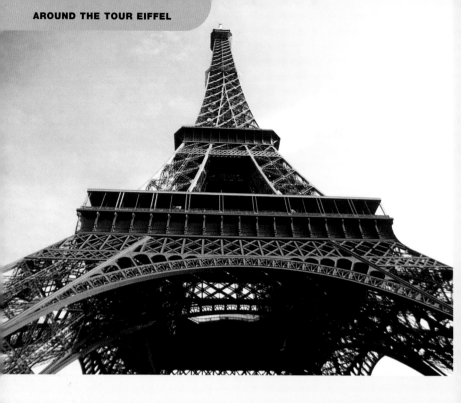

the tower was proved to sway just 6.7cm (2.6 inches). The lattice pattern of ironwork was designed to enable the tower to withstand strong winds.

The structure is an astonishing feat of engineering. It is 125m (410 feet) at its widest point, and 324m (1,063 feet) high, with a series of three platforms to break the long trek of 1,665 steps to the top, although lifts make for an easier and quicker journey. It has more than 18,000 individual metal parts, weighs 10,000 tonnes in total, and comprises 2.5 million rivets. It takes no less than 60 tonnes of paint to redecorate it, which takes place every seven to ten years.

A total of 20,000 light bulbs illuminate the tower for 10 minutes at the beginning of every hour, with spotlights on the ground capturing its latticework structure. A lighted beacon rotates at its highest point.

A visit to the top provides a panoramic view of the city, and on a clear day you can see to a distance of over 60km (37 miles). However, be prepared for queues for the lifts as most visitors prefer not to walk up all those steps. A good tip is to take the steps to the first floor and hop on to the elevator at this point, or go after dark when there are fewer people about. The view of Paris at night from its base is one that will remain in your memory, and is an experience that probably eclipses a daylight view. There is a restaurant on the second level where you can have a meal while enjoying the views. A museum on the first level records the history of the tower, including information on famous people who have visited it.

Above: The Tour Eiffel viewed from beneath, soaring into the sky

Tour Montparnasse

The view from the top of the 59-storey Tour Montparnasse is without a doubt the best in Paris. Apart from the breathtaking skyline of the city in front of you, you actually have the sense of looking down on the Tour Eiffel. Curiously, the Tour Montparnasse is a mere 210m (689 feet) tall compared to the Tour Eiffel's 324m (1,063 feet), but the latter's shape helps in creating this illusion.

The tower was built to a modernist design between 1969 and 1972 and is located on top of the Montparnasse-Bienvenue Paris metro station in the Montparnasse square. Dominating the skyline of the Left Bank, it is essentially an office block, and one of the tallest in Europe. However, as a tourist attraction it is a must-see, if only for the view. A gallery on the 56th floor and a terrace on the 59th floor, which can be reached by a lift in just 38 seconds, are good vantage points. On a clear day it is possible to see aeroplanes taking off at Orly airport 40km (25 miles) away.

Left: A spectacular view from the top of the Tour Montparnasse

✚ **17 off map at E3**

✉ **Tour Montparnasse**
33 avenue du Maine

☎ 01 45 38 5256

www **www.tourmont parnasse56.com**

◷ Summer 9:30am–11pm; winter 9:30am–10:30pm; Fri, Sat and day before pubic holidays until 11pm

✋ Moderate

🚇 Montparnasse-Bienvenue

Latin Quarter, St-Germain & Islands

During the 19th and 20th centuries, Paris' intellectual elite, its writers and prominent artists, created the city's fashionable café society – a legacy that thrives even today. Full of art galleries, bookshops, restaurants and street entertainers, the Latin Quarter and St-Germain are especially lively cultural areas of the city. The nearby Île de la Cité, site of the great Notre Dame cathedral, is usually teeming with life and is, historically and indisputably, the very heart of Paris.

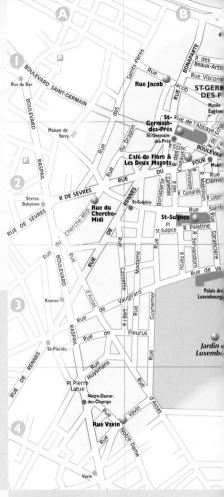

LATIN QUARTER AND ST-GERMAIN WALK

1. Conciergerie
See page 46
Starting in the Boulevard du Palais, take a look at the Conciergerie building. Its conical towers and austere façade dominate the banks of the River Seine at this point. Around 2,800 people were held here during the French Revolution. From here walk along the Quai de la Corse, right into rue de la Cité Notre-Dame and to the cathedral.

2. Notre-Dame
See page 62
The extraordinary building of Notre-Dame de Paris took over 180 years (1163–1345) to complete. Admire it from the square in front, take a walk around its perimeter, and then go inside for an astonishing view. From here, cross the river and take the rue Saint-Jacques, right to boulevard Saint-Germain and the Musée National de Cluny.

3. Musée National de Cluny
See page 60
One of the finest medieval buildings in Paris, this imposing mansion is surrounded by centuries-old, heavily landscaped gardens, and houses a remarkable collection of textiles, tapestries, paintings, wood carvings and other artefacts from day-to-day life. From here, take the boulevard Saint-Michel to the Jardin du Luxembourg.

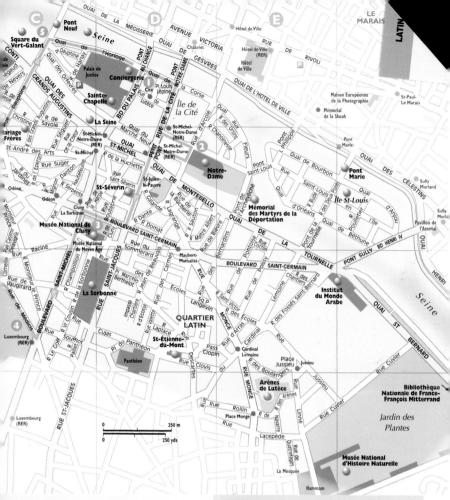

LE MARAIS

LATIN

Square du Vert-Galant

Pont Neuf

QUAI DE LA MÉGISSERIE

AVENUE VICTORIA

Hôtel de Ville

Hôtel de Ville (RER)

DE RIVOLI

Seine

QUAI DE L'HORLOGE

QUAI DES GESVRES

Châtelet

Hôtel de Ville

Palais de Justice

Conciergerie

Sainte-Chapelle

Cité

Pl Louis Lépine

Île de la Cité

QUAI DE L'HOTEL DE VILLE

Maison Européenne de la Photographie

St-Paul-Le Marais

La Seine

Mémorial de la Shoah

QUAI DES GRANDS AUGUSTINS

Marché Neuf

La Corse

Quai d'Arcole

QUAI St-MICHEL

St-Michel-Notre-Dame (RER)

St-Michel

Île St-Louis

Pont Marie

QUAI DES CÉLESTINS

Sully Morland

St-Séverin

R de la Huchette

St-Julien-le-Pauvre

Notre-Dame

QUAI DE MONTEBELLO

Mémorial des Martyrs de la Déportation

Île St-Louis

Quai d'Anjou

Sully Morland

Pavillon de l'Arsenal

Musée National de Cluny

Musée National du Moyen Age

BOULEVARD SAINT-GERMAIN

QUAI DE LA TOURNELLE

Institut du Monde Arabe

Seine

La Sorbonne

BOULEVARD SAINT-GERMAIN

QUARTIER LATIN

St-Étienne-du-Mont

Luxembourg (RER)

Panthéon

Place Jussieu

Jussieu

QUAI St BERNARD

Bibliothèque Nationale de France-François Mitterrand

Luxembourg (RER)

Arènes de Lutèce

Jardin des Plantes

Place Monge

Musée National d'Histoire Naturelle

La Mosquée

Hammam

0   250 m
0   250 yds

---

4. Jardin du Luxembourg
See page 56

These beautifully landscaped gardens date from the 17th century, with English designs added in the early 19th century. They are a peaceful and welcome stop to enjoy the atmosphere of this lively area of Paris. Now take one of the roads signposted to the Île de la Cité, cross the boulevard Saint-Germain and head for the quayside and the Pont Neuf.

5. Pont Neuf
See page 67

Connecting the Left Bank with the Right Bank via the Île de la Cité, the Pont Neuf is the oldest bridge in Paris. It caused a great controversy when it was built in the 16th century as it had no residential buildings. From here the towers of the Conciergerie can be seen, thus completing a walk of the Latin Quarter and St-Germain.

Arènes de Lutèce

In stark contrast to the elegant 17th-century architecture that typifies most of the buildings of Paris, the Arènes de Lutèce is a good deal older. An amphitheatre that was all but destroyed in AD 280, although restored in the early 1900s, it is the only Gallo-Roman remains surviving in Paris other than those at the Thermes de Cluny. It was built between the 1st and the end of the 2nd century.

Bibliothèque Nationale de France – François Mitterrand

With four glass towers at each corner designed to resemble open books, this spacious and bright new library on the Left Bank can be a little intimidating at first sight. However, step inside and a wealth of literature and media awaits you. It has around 12 million books stored in towers, along with a massive collection of documents, videos, CDs and DVDs that attract students as well as visitors to the city. A central courtyard overlooks the Seine.

Below: Playing boules near the Arènes de Lutèce
far below: The building blocks of the Bibliothèque Nationale dominate the skyline

Arènes de Lutèce

✚ 43 E4

✉ **Arènes de Lutèce**
47 rue Monge

🌐 **www.paris.balades.com**

🕐 Summer 8am–10pm; winter 8–5

✋ Free

🚇 Cardinal-Lemoine, Jussieu

Bibliothèque Nationale de France – François Mitterrand

✚ 43 off map at F4

✉ **Bibliothèque Nationale de France-François Mitterrand**
quai François-Mauriac

☎ 01 53 79 59 59

🌐 **www.bnf.fr**

🕐 Tue–Sat 10–8, Sun 1–7

✋ Inexpensive

🚇 Bibliothèque François-Mitterrand

Café de Flore

With its red seating, mirrors and mahogany fittings that have changed little since World War II, the Café de Flore is not so much an eating establishment as a Parisian institution. Its extraordinary art deco interior takes you a step back in time. Situated just off the boulevard Saint-Germain, it has long been a favourite haunt of artisans and intellectuals. Indeed, some even believe that the ghosts of Simone de Beauvoir and Jean-Paul Sartre, who frequented the café, still make the odd appearance.

Today, the Café de Flore is a great place to sit, enjoy a light lunch, and people-watch, albeit at a more than moderate price. It still attracts literary types, and is known for the Prix de Flore, a prize given each year to written works of note. The prize was the brainchild of writer Frédéric Beigbeder and was launched with much fanfare in 1994.

Above: Inside the Café de Flore, a place with a long literary tradition on the boulevard St-Germain

✚ 42 B2

✉ Café de Flore
172 boulevard Saint-Germain

☎ 01 45 48 55 26

🌐 www.cafe-de-flore.com

🕐 Daily 7:30am–1:30am

✋ Expensive

Ⓜ St-Germain-des-Prés

Conciergerie

If the French Revolution is a period of history that fascinates you, then a trip to the Conciergerie is a must. This former palace became Paris' first prison, where thousands were jailed in the late 18th century, most of whom were executed by guillotine.

The building has a dramatic, if unpleasant past. Its most prominent resident was Queen Marie Antoinette, but it also held George Danton, a lawyer involved in the removal of the royal court from Versailles, the romantic poet André Chénier, in later years, and Madame Elizabeth, mistress of Napoleon III. Marie Antoinette's cell is now a chapel to her memory.

The building, with its spiked conical-shaped towers and austere grey façade, stands a trifle gloomily in the complex of the Palais de Justice on the Île de la Cité. It was built in the 14th century as a palace for King Philip IV, but was turned into a prison when the royal family moved to the nearby Louvre. High-ranking prisoners, such as Marie Antoinette, were given their own cells with a few comforts, while common criminals shared damp, dark cells known as *oubliettes,* or 'forgotten places'. It is said that many were tortured within its walls, creating fear among the residents of Paris that lasted for decades.

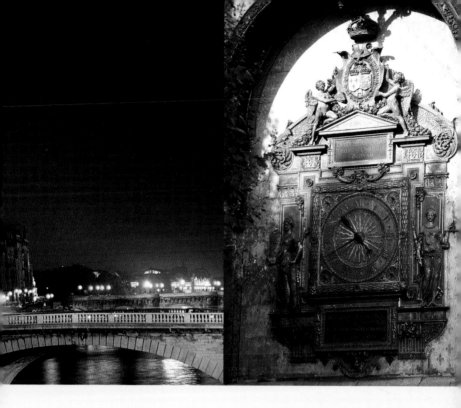

The Conciergerie ceased to be a prison in 1914, and became a centre of Paris' legal system, housing the law courts. At the same time it was declared a national historical monument and was opened to the public.

Visitors enter through the boulevard du Palais entrance and immediately set foot into the Salle des Gens d'Armes. One of the best-preserved Gothic-style medieval halls in Europe, this room would have been used by the royal household as a place to dine. From here, a tour takes you to the Galerie des Prisonniers, which contains a re-creation of the Salle de Toilette, where prisoners were prepared for execution.

Above: The ornate 14th-century clock on the tower is the city's oldest clock and it is still working

✚ **43 D1**

✉ **Conciergerie**
boulevard du Palais

☎ 01 53 40 60 80

🕐 Summer 9:30–6; winter 9–5

✋ Moderate

🚇 Cité, Châtelet boulevard du Palais

Above left: A view at night, across the river, of La Conciergerie, a prison during the French Revolution

Les Deux Magots

Names from the world of literature and art – Simone de Beauvoir, Jean-Paul Sartre, Ernest Hemingway and Pablo Picasso, to name a few – are linked with this café in the Saint-Germain-des-Prés area, a popular spot for street entertainers such as mime artists and musicians.

✚ 42 B2

✉ **Les Deux Magots**
170 boulevard Saint-Germain

☎ 01 45 48 55 25

🌐 **www.lesdeuxmagots.fr**

🕐 Daily 7:30am–1:30am

🚇 St-Germain-des-Prés

Les Deux Magots has gained a reputation for attracting larger than life characters from the Paris elite, and is an ideal spot to take in the atmosphere and watch people go by.

The café, which takes its unusual name from two statues of Chinese commercial agents (*magots*) that feature among its decor, lends its name to the Les Deux Magots literary prize, a prestigious award that has been handed out each year since 1933 and which is eagerly sought by many French authors.

Above: Les Deux Magots is a very popular streetside café on boulevard St-Germain, which used to be a favourite haunt of intellectuals

Église Saint-Étienne-du-Mont

This church on the Holy Genevieve mound in the Latin Quarter, just a short walk from rue Saint-Jacques and the Sorbonne, has an extraordinary combination of architectural styles.

Parts of the church date back to the 15th century. Later additions include the bells, which were cast in 1500, and the choral areas, stained-glass windows and chapels, built right through to the 1600s when the pulpit was added. Its Gothic, Renaissance and classical styles merge beautifully together. Inside, it has a rare, richly carved wooden screen over the nave.

The church has enjoyed some importance over the centuries, particularly during the 16th and 17th centuries when it was frequented by notable Parisians. Among the many popes who have been here were Pope Pie VII in 1805 and Pope Jean-Paul II in 1997.

Above: The unique carved rood-screen snakes over the nave in the Église Saint-Étienne-du-Mont

✚ **43 D3**

✉ **Église Saint-Étienne-du-Mont**
place Sainte-Genevieve

☎ 01 43 54 11 79

🕐 Tue–Sat 8–noon, 2–7, Sun 9–noon, 2:30–7

🎫 Free

Ⓜ Cardinal Lemoine

Église Saint-Germain-des-Prés

This handsome Romanesque-style church has the distinction of being one of Paris' oldest surviving ecclesiastical buildings. Parts of it date back to the 10th century.

In those days the Saint-Germain-des-Prés district, where the church is located, would have been outside the city and, as such, would have had to be fortified against attack. Since the church was a natural target it was built with a wall and a moat to guard it. Several watch towers were added, but only one, the largest, constructed in the 11th century, survives.

In the 19th century the church underwent extensive restoration and today displays many examples of classic 19th-century architecture, including a series of stained-glass windows depicting scenes from the Old Testament. The serene and peaceful surroundings of the church provide a tranquil retreat away from busy St-Germain.

Below: The majestic interior of St-Germain-des-Prés

✚ **42 B2**

✉ **Église Saint-Germain-des-Prés**
3 place Saint-Germain-des-Prés

☎ 01 55 42 81 33

🕐 Mon–Sat 8–7,
Sun 9–7

💵 Free

Ⓜ St-Germain-des-Prés

Église Saint-Séverin

This church is one of the city's finest examples of Gothic architecture and dominates the lively cultural area immediately around the Église Saint-Séverin. It has an unusually styled steeple that contains one of Paris' oldest bells, dating from the 15th century.

Standing on the site of an important 11th-century church, the Église Saint-Séverin mainly dates from the 12th and 13th centuries. It has long provided religious instruction to the residents of the area. Numerous gargoyles are a feature of the external design, while inside, a series of richly coloured stained-glass windows tells the story of Saint Séverin,

a hermit who prayed in a chapel on the site of the church. The architecture of the Chapelle Mansart and the pillars carved in the fashion of palm trees are of note. Another outstanding feature is the marble choir funded by the Duchess of Montpensier, a cousin of King Louis XIV.

Above: Look up to see the characteristic gargoyles

✚ **43 D2**

✉ **Église Saint-Séverin**
rue des Prêtres Saint-Séverin

☎ 01 42 34 93 50

🌐 **www.saint-severin.com**

🕐 Daily 11–7:30,
Sun 9–7

🎟 Free

🚇 Saint-Michel, Notre-Dame

Église Saint-Sulpice

This dramatic church is probably the finest example of classical asymmetrical 17th-century French architecture in an ecclesiastical building in Paris. Much of the work seen on the present-day church took more than 130 years to complete and was the creation of several prominent architects of the day, such as Christophe Garnard, Louis Vau and Daniel Gittard.

The walls of the church carry a stunning array of artworks, most notably frescoes by Delacroix, including his *Jacob Wrestling with the Angel* in the Chapel of the Angels, and 19th-century works by Victor Mottez and Jacques-Emile Lafon.

The François-Henri Clicquot organ was built between 1776 and 1781, and is one of the largest in Europe. It is surrounded by statues by François Dumont.

Right: The Église Saint-Sulpice has a beautiful fountain at its entrance

 42 B2

⊠ **Église Saint-Sulpice**
place Saint-Sulpice

☎ 01 46 33 21 78

🕐 Mon–Sat 8:30–7:15, Sun 8:30–7:45

✋ Free

🚇 Saint-Sulpice

Île Saint-Louis

This small island in the heart of Paris, which you can reach via the Pont Marie, the Pont de la Tournelle, the Pont L Phillippe or the Pont Saint-Louis, is often overlooked in favour of its much larger neighbour, the Île de la Cité. Since it is a fashionable place to live, it is also one of the city's most expensive areas, and full of character, with stately 18th-century houses that are home to the rich and famous of Paris. Georges Pompidou, the former president of France, lived on the island.

Named after King Louis IX, the island dates from the reigns of Henri IV and Louis XIII, and was designed exclusively for residential use. Take some time to walk around the streets, admire the architecture and enjoy this quiet little haven in the middle of the city. You can view the island from the Seine, too, by taking one of the boat trips.

The 17th-century church of Saint-Louis is worth visiting for its ornate baroque-style interior and an unusual clock on one of the walls.

Above: View along the River Seine from the Île Saint-Louis

+ **43 F2**

☒ **Île Saint-Louis, Church**

🕐 Daily 8–7:30

🎫 Free

🚇 Pont Marie

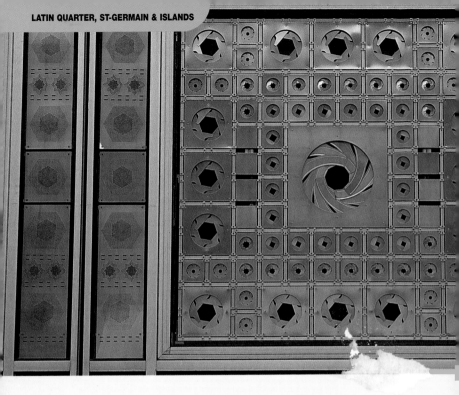

Institut du Monde Arabe

One of the most innovative buildings in Paris is the Institut du Monde Arabe. Great expanses of geometrically patterned glass and aluminium adorn it. It was built in 1987 by architect Jean Nouvel (and Architecture Studio), whose aim was to create a monument that displayed a synergy between Arab and Western culture. It was approved by François Mitterrand, who wanted to create modern landmarks for the city of Paris.

The northernmost façade faces the historic heart of Paris and its futuristic design is meant to echo Western thinking. The side facing the south features metal screens in Islamic geometric style that change dramatically with the light. A series of diaphragms open and close throughout the day, and a book tower in white marble seen through the glass evokes images of the minarets of traditional mosques.

The building houses the Arab World Institute, which aims to raise awareness and understanding of Arabic culture through workshops, language courses, and science and technology exhibitions that are open to the public.

A large museum within the institute contains works from French national museums, along with items such as flint tools, textiles, mosaics, stuccoes,

jewels, ceramics, carpets, calligraphy and metalwork from Algeria, Saudi Arabia, Bahrain, Comoros, Djibouti, Egypt, United Arab Emirates, Iraq, Jordan, Kuwait, Lebanon, Libya, Morocco, Mauritania, Oman, Palestine, Qatar, Somalia, the Sudan and Yemen.

There is also a display of 184 objects, from prehistoric times to the 18th century, donated by Syria and Tunisia, the first two countries to participate in the establishment of the institute. A library and a bookshop contain a wide selection of books on Arab culture and Islamic thought in French, along with around 65,000 works in French and Arabic on subjects ranging from religion and philosophy to literature and history. An audio-visual room contains photographs, documents and music, and has continuous film screenings of events, past and present, from Arab countries.

✚ **43 E3**

✉ **Institut du Monde Arab**
   1 rue des Fossés Saint-Bernard

☎ 01 40 51 38 38

🌐 **www.imarabe.org**

🕐 Tue–Sun 10–6

✋ Inexpensive

Ⓜ Jussieu, Cardinal Lemoine

Jardin du Luxembourg

The largest gardens in the city are usually packed with walkers, joggers and picnickers, people reading, children playing, flower enthusiasts and dog-walkers. The Jardin du Luxembourg is one of the busiest gardens in the city yet somehow remains a relaxing place to go.

Designed by Salomon de Brosse, who was commissioned by Marie de Médicis, wife of Henri IV, to create a garden that resembled her childhood Florentine home, the Jardin du Luxembourg was started in 1615, and took almost 12 years to complete. Although one area was laid out in the English style, the garden is the epitome of French landscaping, with walkways and classically designed planted areas. It forms part of the magnificent Palais du Luxembourg, home of the French Senate. The great Allée de l'Observatoire walkway was added in the 19th century.

Shrubs and flowers blend with chestnut and palm trees, which are occasionally interrupted by fountains, including the great Médicis fountain, and there is a bandstand and sculptures, including a row depicting the queens of France and famous Parisian

writers and artists. A small-scale replica of the Statue of Liberty (the original was a gift from France to the USA) stands in a wooded section, while a later addition is an official memorial to the victims of the 9/11 tragedy. A tree has been planted in their memory, with a plaque to identify it. During World War II, the complex served as the headquarters of the Luftwaffe.

The garden is laid out in a deliberate fashion for ease of use and beauty. A large octagonal pond in front of the Palais du Luxembourg provides a point from where you can drift in any direction along the tree-lined avenues. And if walking does not appeal, just grab a chair and relax. There is also a large playground, complete with carousel rides, a puppet show, and a pond where children can sail toy boats.

✛ **42 B3**

✉ **Jardin du Luxembourg**
boulevard Saint-Michel

☎ Senate 01 42 34 20 00

🌐 **www.senat.fr**

🕓 Apr–end Oct, daily 7:30am–9:30pm; Nov–end Mar, 8:15am–5pm (times can vary)

✋ Free

Ⓜ Odéon

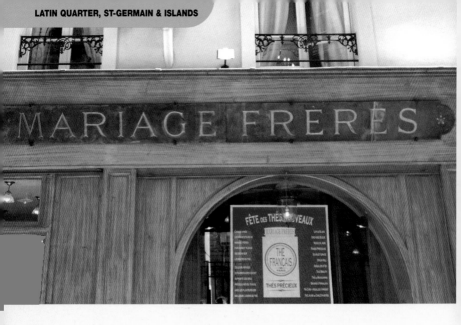

Mariage Frères

For anyone who loves tea, a visit to the world-renowned French tea-blender and purveyor of fine teas, Mariage Frères, is a must. It was founded by the brothers Henri and Edouard Mariage in 1854 and handed down from through the family, generation to generation. There are two stylish centres of tea where visitors sit back in the supremely elegant surroundings, and choose from around 600 different varieties on offer.

⊞ 43 C2

✉ Mariage Frères
rue des Grands-Augustins;
30 rue du Bourg Tibourg

☎ 01 40 51 82 50;
01 42 72 28 11

🖥 www.mariagefreres.com

🕐 Daily 10:30–7:30, tea room noon–7

Ⓜ Odéon, Hotel de Ville

Categorised into broad types – black, green, green flavoured, traditional, herbal, white, and others – the rich variety of teas come from all around the world.

The choice includes Gunpowder Zhu Cha from China, Marco Polo from Tibet and China, the Thè au Sahara from South Africa, and Casablanca, a mint tea from China. The most popular of all is the Wedding Imperial – a golden Assam from India, whose other brands are as sought after as this exclusive one.

Head upstairs in this colonial-style mansion to the chic tea room, complete with palm trees and rattan furniture, and enjoy a tea and patisserie or a light lunch. Many of the recipes are tea based and delicious.

Above: The entrance to Mariage Frères

Mémorial des Martyrs de la Déportation

This is an austere but well-visited memorial to the French citizens who were deported to concentration camps by the Nazis during World War II. It is situated in the shadow of the flying buttresses of Notre Dame, on the banks of the Île de la Cité.

The memorial, designed by G H Pingusson, comprises a crypt, reached by a series of steps. The space was designed deliberately to evoke the miserable conditions in which the unfortunate deportees might have found themselves.

The long corridor is lined with 200,000 quartz pebbles and a small light flickers for each person who failed to return. As you enter, read the plaque to appreciate the enormity of what the memorial commemorates and to understand its symbolism. Each step will be a moving experience.

Above: Part of the Mémorial des Martyrs de la Déportation, which commemorates the French killed during the Holocaust

✚ **43 E2**

✉ **Mémorial des Martyrs de la Déportation** square de l'Île de France

☎ 01 46 33 87 56

🌐 **www.paris.org**

🕐 Apr–Oct, daily 10–noon, 2–7; Nov–Mar, 10–noon, 2–5

💶 Free

Ⓜ Cité

Musée National de Cluny

This is one of the treasures of Paris that every visitor should see. Dating from the 1500s and built to designs inspired by the Abbot Jacques d'Amboise, the museum is beautifully preserved and one of the finest examples of 16th-century domestic architecture in France. It has changed little over the centuries, and transports visitors back to a fascinating era.

Gothic turrets herald your approach to the mansion, surrounded by re-created medieval gardens giving off a heady scent of flowers. Inside, a collection of approximately 23,000 items, amassed largely by Alexandre du Sommerard, a 19th-century collector of medieval memorabilia, features tapestries, costumes, textiles and metals from several continents. Many of the textiles and tapestries are European or Byzantine. Some of the most mesmerising pieces include *La Dame à la Licorne*, woven in the 1400s and one of the world's most famous tapestries from that period.

Jewels and artefacts made of gold and other metals, including a magnificent glistening altar front, originate from Gallic, Barbarian, Merovingian and Visigothic eras. Notice the Visigothic votive crown, and an Averbode altarpiece. There is also a seemingly endless collection of books, manuscripts, ceramics, wood carvings and religious items. And do not miss the collection of exquisite stained glass.

The Musée National de Cluny is famed for being the site of the Roman Baths in the adjoining Hôtel de Cluny. Dating from the 2nd century ad and in remarkably good condition, the baths comprise three chambers: the steam room, known as the Caldarium; the tepid bath or Tepidarium, and the Frigidarium, or cold bath. Roman architecture is still in evidence, such as the labyrinth of vaulted rooms, and the remains of a gymnasium.

✚ 43 C2

✉ Musée National de Cluny
place Paul-Painlevé

☎ 01 53 73 78 00

🖰 www.musee-moyenage.fr

🕐 Wed–Mon 9:15–5:45

💶 Moderate

🚇 Cluny-La Sorbonne

Above: Exterior of the Musée de Cluny, which is also known as the Musée National du Moyen Age

Musée National d'Histoire Naturelle

This museum traces its roots back to 1793. It contains an outstanding collection of exhibits on mineralogy, geology, palaeontology and comparative anatomy in separate museums within its compound, and also has a fascinating botanical garden and zoo. It lies within the Jardin des Plantes, where the Royal Garden of Medicinal Plants, laid out in 1635, is a refreshingly quiet place to jog, walk, or simply sit and enjoy a book.

The Grande Galerie de l'Évolution is one of the fascinating museums. It has exhibits on the evolution of animals, the diversity of living species known to man, as well as those that are extinct or in danger of extinction. The Ménagerie, one of the world's oldest zoological gardens, has bird and reptile collections in their re-created natural environments, along with many varieties of plants.

Above: A visitor enjoys the tranquillity of the Jardin des Plantes, a fine setting for the museum

🏠 43 F4

✉ **Musée National d'Histoire Naturelle**
Jardin des Plantes, 57 rue Cuvier

☎ 01 40 79 56 01

🌐 www.mnhn.fr

🕐 Gardens daily; Grand Galerie de l'Évolution Wed–Mon 10–6; Ménagerie summer 9–6, winter 9–5; closed bank holidays; other exhibitions Wed–Mon 10–5, Sun and pubic holidays 10–6

💷 Moderate, gardens free

🚇 Jussieu, Gare-d'Austerlitz

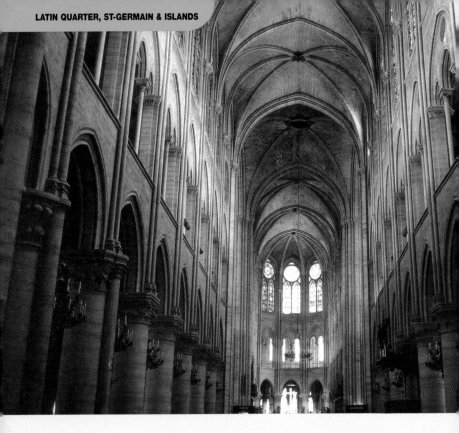

Notre-Dame

One of the greatest buildings ever built, Notre-Dame stands proudly on the Île de la Cité. The seat of the Archbishop of Paris, it is the spiritual heart of the city, and indeed, of the country. The cathedral is an outstanding example of 12th- to 14th-century master craftsmanship and an architectural marvel. It is characterised by flying buttresses, gargoyles, a spire that stands some 90m (295 feet) tall, towers that offer the visitor a panoramic view of the city, and its grand west wing.

Work started on the building in 1163 based on Bishop Maurice de Sully's dazzling design, with Pope Alexander III laying the first stone, However, the construction was not completed until around 1345. Architectural styles changed significantly over the span of years during which it was being built and the result was a cathedral with both Gothic and Romanesque influences. The choir was completed in 1182, the nave in 1208, and the bell, called Emmanuel, was cast in 1631.

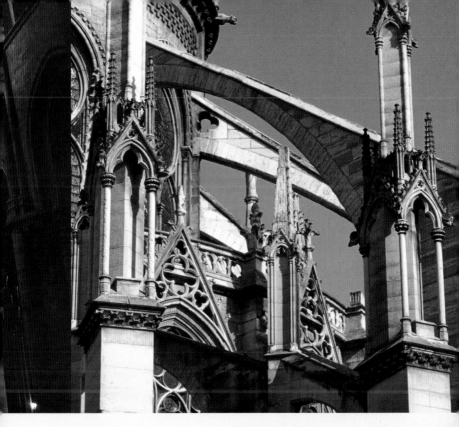

The west wing façade and the main entrance to the cathedral is probably its most photographed feature. Comprising three exquisitely carved portals with biblical scenes representing the life of Saint Anne, the story of the Last Judgement and the Virgin, and a row of statues above known as the Kings' Gallery, the wing features a beautifully preserved stained-glass rose window for which Notre-Dame is world renowned. The window dates back to the early Gothic period, although two other

Above left: The 35m (115-foot) high nave of the church is a stunning example of Gothic architecture
Above right: A splendid view of the flying buttresses at the east end of Notre-Dame

✚ **43 D2**

✉ **Notre-Dame**
place du Parvis de Notre Dame,
Île de la Cité

☎ 01 42 34 45 10; crypt 01 55 42 50 10;
museum 01 43 25 42 92

🌐 **www.paris.org**

🕐 Mon–Sat 8–6:45, Sun 8–7:45; crypt
daily 10–6 except Mon; museum
Wed, Sat and Sun 2:30–6

✋ Cathedral and museum free, crypt
inexpensive

🚇 Cité, St-Michel

Far left: The famed rose window parapet depicting the Virgin and Child flanked by angels
Left: Rear view of Notre Dame
Above: Candles burn continuously in the cathedral

windows on the north and south are older and date from about 1250–60.

The cathedral's interior is essentially Romanesque in style, with influences of naturalism that give it a livelier appearance. It houses softly lit chapels, numerous statues – including the celebrated statue of the Virgin and Child – and tombs, carved out of a softly coloured stone.

Look out for the sacristy. It is here that many of the city's ancient manuscripts are kept. In the archaeological crypt, the most important in Europe, the remains of Gallo-Roman to 18th-century foundations can be seen. A display shows Parisian life on the Île de la Cité from the 3rd to the 19th century.

Notre-Dame was almost destroyed during the French Revolution, and underwent a major renovation in the 19th century under the direction of medievalist architect, Viollet-le-Duc.

Pont Marie

A handsome, sturdy bridge comprising a series of five stone arches, the Pont Marie connects the Île Saint-Louis with the Right Bank at the quai des Célestins, and is one of the city's oldest bridges. It combines classical architecture with Renaissance influences, and was named after the property developer who worked on the project. King Louis XIII commissioned the bridge and laid the first stone in 1614, with the work taking about 30 years to complete.

✚ **43 F2**

✉ **Pont Marie**
   quai des Célestins

🕐 24 hours

✋ Free

🚇 Pont Marie

The bridge was designed to accommodate dwellings of several storeys in height, and, indeed, they stood here for a great many years, until a large number of them were destroyed by floods in the late 18th century. Those that remained were declared unsafe and were demolished in 1788. This meant, of course, that several families who had made the bridge their home had to be accommodated elsewhere. The bridge underwent a restoration programme in 1850, and is today widely used and admired for its historic importance.

Above: A distant view of the Pont Marie

Pont Neuf

Despite its name, which means New Bridge, the Pont Neuf is the oldest surviving bridge in Paris. The arched structure, 278m (910 feet) long, spans the Seine and connects the Île de la Cité with the Right Bank at quai de la Mégisserie, and the Left Bank at quai de Conti. There are 12 arches in all, built to a classical Renaissance style.

The bridge dates from around 1578 to 1607, and caused much controversary at the time because, unlike the usual design for such structures of the day, it did not feature rows of houses. It preceded the pedestrianised bridges we now regard as a necessity for any city.

It was commissioned by King Henri III, who never lived to see its completion. On its inauguration in 1607, the king, Henri IV, is said to have ridden across the bridge at some speed. Indeed, the bridge bore a commemorative statue of the king on horseback, commissioned by his widow, Marie de Médicis. This stood for several centuries until it was melted down during the French Revolution. The statue was replaced in 1818.

Major restoration works were completed in 2007, the 400th anniversary of the bridge's unveiling.

Above: From Pont Neuf there are wonderful views of the Tour Eiffel

✚ **43 C1**

✉ **Pont Neuf**
quai de la Mégisserie

🕐 24 hours

🖐 Free

🚇 Pont Neuf

Rue du Cherche-Midi

A walk along the rue du Cherche-Midi will reveal some of the finest 18th-century domestic buildings in the city. Tall structures display a classic line of elaborately carved façade, arched windows and Juliet-style balconies. A statue of a centaur by the French sculptor César stands at one end. This street is home to many Parisians, and is also the location for several fine specialist shops that have replaced the antiques merchants for which the street was once famous.

The renowned Poilâne bakery is at No 8, where all kinds of cakes, bread, biscuits and pastries make for a lavish, and extremely tempting, window display. The bakery is just a few doors away from the Musée Hébert, a museum dedicated to the work of painter Ernest Hébert, and housed in a former 18th-century hotel, the Hôtel de Montmorency, at No 85. A fashionable portraitist, Hébert was the official painter of the Second Empire and went on to become a director of the Academy of France in Rome. In his honour, the museum displays notable examples of his work.

✚ **42 A2**

✉ **Rue du Cherche-Midi**

🚇 St-Sulpice

Above: This famous patisserie displays a mouthwatering range of artisan-baked bread and pastries

Rue Jacob

Set in the heart of the cultural area of St-Germain-des-Prés, the rue Jacob is the ideal place to while away a few hours as you explore the area. It is also a short walk from the banks of the River Seine via the rue Bonaparte and the Musée National Eugène Delacroix, which contains works by the great French painter.

The street is a great place for window shopping at the fascinating shops brimming with antiques, or those that specialise in interior design and decorative items.

Rue Vavin, No 26

Located in one of the more picturesque streets, rue Vavin, and within a reasonable walk from the Tour Montparnasse in one direction and the Jardin du Luxembourg in the other, this property stands out from its neighbouring classic 18th-century properties because of its unusually decorated front façade. It has a series of stepped balconies adorned with blue and white ceramic tiles, not dissimilar to those found

on some Dutch houses. The building is known as the "Sporting House with Steps".

Above: Paris is famous for its patisseries, such as this one in rue Jacob

---

✚ **42 B1**

✉ **Rue Jacob**

🚇 Vavin

✚ **42 A4**

✉ **Rue Vavin, No 26**

🚇 Vavin

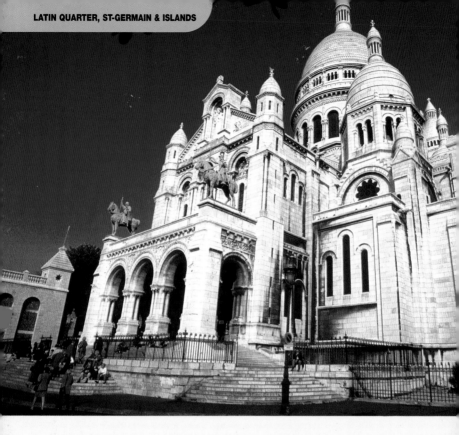

Sainte-Chapelle

A Gothic masterpiece, widely regarded as the city's most beautiful church, the Sainte-Chapelle is famed for its exquisite stained-glass windows. It was called the "gateway to heaven" in medieval times, and is a breathtaking sight with the magical quality of light that filters in.

The Sainte-Chapelle was built in the 13th century on direction from King Louis IX, who became Saint Louis, in order to provide a safe house for the many holy relics he had acquired during the Crusades. These included what is widely believed to be Christ's Crown of Thorns, purchased from Beaudouin II, the Emperor of Constantinople, in 1239, along with drops of Christ's blood and fragments of the Cross. The church became, and remains, a significant religious building.

The work was designed by Pierre de Montreuil, and became Louis IX's private chapel, a stone's throw away from the royal palace, in 1248. It is famed for its masterly architecture, both inside and on the exterior. Heavily damaged during the French Revolution, it underwent restoration under medievalist architect Viollet-le-Duc in 1840.

Above: Intricate carvings inside the upper chapel of the church

Today, the church retains its reputation for the magnificence of its 15 stained-glass windows and the large rose window. Most of these date from the 13th century, making them the oldest of their kind in Paris. There are more than 1,000 biblical scenes depicted in the windows, starting with the Genesis and culminating with St John's vision of the Apocalypse, in the rose window. The latter is made up of 86 different panels. The building also features a star-covered vaulted roof and an important collection of wall paintings.

Above left: Completed in 1248, the Sainte-Chapelle is one of the oldest monuments in Paris

✚ **43 D1**

✉ **Sainte-Chapelle**
boulevard du Palais

☎ 01 53 40 60 80

W·W·W **www.monuments-nationaux.fr**

🕐 Daily 9:30–6

✋ Moderate

🚇 Cité, St-Michel

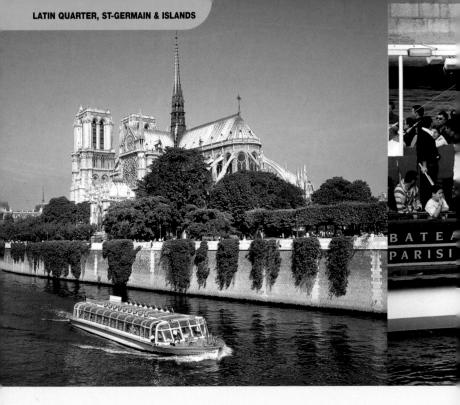

La Seine Boat Trip

One of the most pleasurable ways to see Paris is from the waters of the Seine. A number of companies run river cruises, almost all with commentary during the day, and most offer romantic after-dark trips lasting several hours that reveal the city in a different perspective. The most coveted place is on the top deck during an evening cruise, from where you can admire the subtly lit monuments, while inside you can enjoy a three- or four-course meal and fine wine inside.

Starting points vary; some companies start from lower quayside locations close to the Musée du Louvre, others closer to the Tour Eiffel. Typically, a cruise starting at the Port de la Bourdonnais and heading west will pass under a series of bridges, such as the Pont d'léna, with the Tour Eiffel to the left and the Palais de Chaillot and Jardins du Trocadéro to the right, and the two-tier Pont de Bir-Hakeim before turning back along the Seine in an easterly direction.

The cruise will then follow a route under the Pont de l'Alma and the beautiful Pont Alexandre III, with its four gilded bronze

winged horses at either end. Look to the right and glimpse the gold dome of Les Invalides, while to the left stand the Grand Palais and the Petit Palais. From here, the boat will pass under the Pont de la Concorde, with the Place de la Concorde, although not really visible, to the left, and under the wooden structure of the Passerelle Solférino. A spectacular view of the Musée du Louvre on the left will now start to emerge.

Passing under the Pont Royal, the Pont du Carrousel and the Pont des Arts, one of the most romantic bridges in Paris, and on to the ancient Pont Neuf, where the river meets the Île de la Cité and divides, the boat takes a route past the cathedral of Notre-Dame and on to the Île Saint-Louis, before making a turn and following the route back to the starting point.

Above left: A view of Notre-Dame from across the River Seine
Above: Cruises are popular and the boats are usually quite full

✚ **43 C1**

✉ **La Seine Boat Trips**
Bateaux Mouches: Pont de l'Alma; Bateaux Parisiens Tour Eiffel: Port de la Bourdonnais

☎ 01 42 25 96 10; 01 44 11 33 44

🌐 **www.bateaux-mouches.fr; www.bateauxparisiens.com**

Ⓜ Pont de l'Alma, Trocadéro, Bir-Hakeim

La Sorbonne

Paris' great university started life in 1257 as a humble place of learning for a handful of poor students who wanted to study theology. As the original college expanded, the premises became the permanent home of the University of Paris. Among its alumni were the 13th- to 14th-century Italian poet Dante and the 16th-century church reformer John Calvin.

🔲 **43 C3**

✉ **La Sorbonne**
rue Saint-Jacques

☎ 01 40 46 22 11

🌐 **www.sorbonne.fr**

🕐 Guided tours Mon–Fri 9:30am and 2:30pm by advance booking only

✋ Moderate

Ⓜ Cluny-La Sorbonne

The Sorbonne University is named after Robert de Sorbon, confessor to King Louis IX and founder of the medieval college that became the university.

It was closed during the French Revolution. After extensive renovations and additions in the 19th century, it re-opened in 1809 under the instructions of Napoleon. Today, it is part of an impressive cluster of buildings in the heart of the Latin Quarter, which house a number of colleges that, collectively, form the University of Paris, and include the Collège de France and Lycée Louis-le-Grand.

The university's church is open to the public during special occasions, when you can see the marble tomb of the great Cardinal Richelieu.

Above: Students relax in the place de la Sorbonne

Square du Vert-Galant

Located on the westernmost tip of the Île de la Cité, a short walk from the Palais de Justice buildings, this pretty square is popular with artists and photographers as it offers some of the best views of Paris across the river.

In one direction there is the Pont Neuf, the city's oldest bridge, but the best view overlooks the great riverside façade of the Louvre with the bridges Pont des Arts, Pont du Carrousel, the Pont Royal and the Passerelle Solférino, in its shadow.

This pretty square was created in memory of King Henri IV, a bit of a lady's man, who was aptly nicknamed Vert-Galant, which means "hearty gallant".

The Square du Vert-Galant is a lovely place to rest awhile on one of the benches along its triangular-shaped walled garden. Tall willow trees line the banks of the river, where you can enjoy a picnic lunch.

Above: Water on both sides of the square has a calming effect

🕂 **43 C1**

✉ **Square du Vert-Galant**
place du Pont-Neuf

🕐 Apr–Sep, daily
9am–10:30pm

✋ Free

🚇 Pont Neuf

Marais and Bastille

The Marais and Bastille areas are both lively parts of Paris, each for its own reason. The Marais was once home to the city's aristocracy, as is apparent from the elegant 16th-century mansions that now sit a little uncomfortably with the brightly coloured ultramodern structure of the Centre Georges Pompidou. The Bastille, on the other hand, is more commercial, with chic restaurants, wine bars and art galleries. It also boasts a number of commemorative statues and squares.

77

MARAIS AND BASTILLE WALK

1. Centre Georges Pompidou
See page 81
The extraordinary Centre Georges Pompidou building, with colourful utility pipes outlandishly located on the outside, houses art and film exhibitions. From here, take the rue du Renard towards the river, turning left into the rue de Rivoli to the rue de Fourcy.

2. Maison Européenne de la Photographie
See page 87
Located on the rue de Fourcy, this 18th-century building houses an exceptional collection of contemporary photography over five floors. Take the rue Saint Antoine and turn left into the rue de Birague, past some ornate town houses, to the place des Vosges.

3. Place des Vosges
See page 95
One of the prettiest squares in the city, the place des Vosges is surrounded by the fine architecture of the days when it had a royal palace, pavilions and countless homes of the Paris elite. It links the Marais and Bastille areas. From here, take the rue des Francs-Bourgeois for a short walk to the Musée Carnavalet.

4. Musée Carnavalet
See page 88
The Musée Carnavalet in the rue de Sévigné takes the visitor through different periods, with exhibits from the Bastille prison, Proust's bedroom, and even a picnic bag that once belonged to Napoleon. Head north along rue de Sévigné, then left along rue du Parc Royal and right into rue de Thorigny to the Musée Picasso.

5. Musée Picasso
See page 92
This beautiful 17th-century mansion museum has the largest collection of paintings by Picasso in the world, and works by his favourite painters are also exhibited. To return to the Centre Georges Pompidou, take the rue des Quartre Fils, left into the rue des Archives and right into the rue Rambuteau.

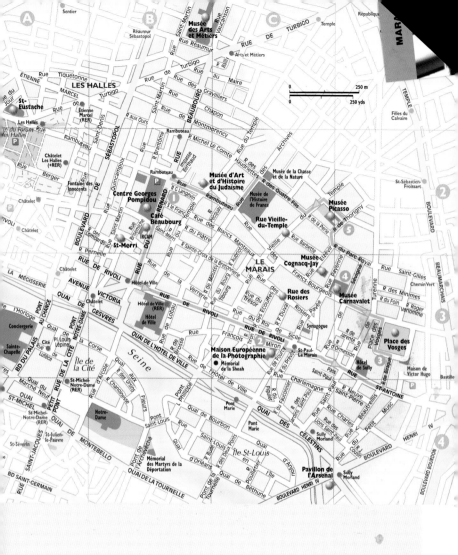

A
Sentier
Rue St-Martin
Rue Vaucanson
B
Musée
des Arts
et Métiers
Rue
République
C
DE
TURBIGO
Temple
MAR...

Réaumur
Sébastopol
Rue Réaumur
Rue de Turbigo
RUE
Temple
DE

Arts et Métiers

Rue
au
Maire
Rue
Bailly
TEMPLE

ÉTIENNE
Rue
Tiquetonne
LES HALLES
MARCEL
Turbigo
Rue
de Turbigo
Rue des
Gravilliers

Rue
Chapon
Filles du
Calvaire

St-
Eustache
Étienne
Marcel (RER)
R aux Ours
Rue St-Martin
Rue Montmorency
Rue du Temple
250 m
0
250 yds

Les Halles
in du Forum
des Halles
Rue du Forum
des Halles
Rambuteau
Rue Michel Le Comte
R des Haudriettes
Archives
St-Sébastien-
Froissart

P
Berger
Rambuteau
R Brantôme
Musée d'Art
et d'Histoire
du Judaïsme
Musée de la Chasse
et de la Nature
2

Châtelet
Les Halles
(+RER)
P
Rambuteau
Rue
R C Langevin
Rambuteau
Musée de
l'Histoire
de France
Temple
Musée
Picasso

Châtelet
Fontaine des
Innocents
Centre Georges
Pompidou
R de France
Rue Vieille-
du-Temple
R de la Perle
R de Thorigny
5
BOULEVARD
BEAUMARCHAIS

TIVOLI
Café
Beaubourg
R St-Merri
Rue des Blancs Manteaux
Vieille
des
R du Parc Royal
Rue
Saint-Gilles
3

Châtelet
St-Merri
IRCAM
R Sainte-Croix de la Bretonnerie
LE
MARAIS
Musée
Cognacq-Jay
Francs-Bourgeois
Rue Barbette
R Payenne
4
Sévigné
Chemin Vert
R des Minimes

LA MÉGISSERIE
AVENUE
VICTORIA
Hôtel de Ville
RUE
DE
RIVOLI
Rue de la
Rue
Verrerie
des
R des
Rosiers
Rue des
Rosiers
Musée
Carnavalet
de
Turenne
R Roger
Verlomme
R du Foin

Conciergerie
Quai
PONT
AU CHANGE
Quai
PI Louis
Lépine
Hôtel de Ville
(RER)
Hôtel
de Ville
RUE
DE
Rue
de Lobau
RIVOLI
RUE
Ecouffes
R Pavée
du Roi
de
Sicile
RUE
DE RIVOLI
Synagogue
de
R de
Jarente
R d'Ormesson
Place des
Vosges
3

Sainte-
Chapelle
Cité
Quai de l'Horloge
Île de
la Cité
Quai de la Corse
Rue François
Miron
St-Paul-
Le Marais
R des Juifs
Hôtel
de Sully
Maison de
Victor Hugo
Bastille
4

St-Michel-
Notre-Dame
(RER)
Lutèce
Quai
aux Fleurs
QUAI DE L'HÔTEL DE VILLE
Maison Européenne
de la Photographie
Mémorial
de la Shoah
R du Pont Louis Philippe
RUE ST-ANTOINE
P

ST-MICHEL
Quai du
Marché Neuf
PETIT PONT
QUAI
St-Michel-
Notre-Dame
(RER)
Rue
d'Arcole
Pont
St-Louis
Quai de Bourbon
Pont
Marie
QUAI
DES
CÉLESTINS
Sully
Morland
Rue Charlemagne
R Neuve
Saint-Pierre
Rue
Saint-Paul
Petit
Musc
HENRI IV

St-Séverin
St-Julien-
le-Pauvre
Notre-
Dame
MONTEBELLO
Pont de
l'Archevêché
Mémorial
des Martyrs
de la Déportation
QUAI DE LA TOURNELLE
Quai
d'Orléans
Île St-Louis
Quai
d'Anjou
Pont
Marie
Rue
Poulletier
Quai
de Béthune
Pavillon de
l'Arsenal
Sully
Morland
BOULEVARD
BOURDON
4

BD SAINT-GERMAIN
BOULEVARD HENRI IV

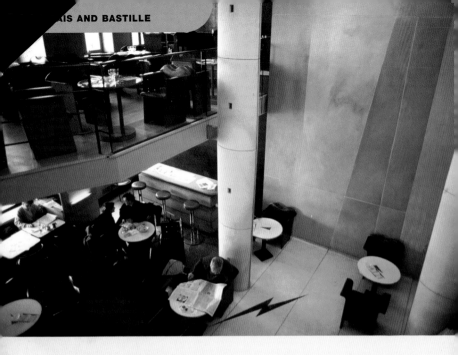

Café Beaubourg

If you want to get a feel of the Parisian cultural scene, visit the ultra-stylish Café Beaubourg. Artists and literary giants rub shoulders with tabloid writers, musicians, poets, critics, marketing executives and trendy young Parisians – all sipping their cocktails and networking furiously. This is where the contemporary fashion and art aficionados hang out.

✚ 79 B2

✉ Café Beaubourg
43 rue Saint-Marri

☎ 01 48 87 63 96

🕐 Daily 8am–1am

🚇 Hôtel de Ville, Châtelet, Rambuteau

The sophisticated café, located right opposite the Centre Georges Pompidou, was designed by Christian de Portzamparc. Its interiors are decorated in neutral creams and browns, dramatically interspersed with splashes of lavish red drapes and stools. Bookcases line some of the walls, while the latest hits play unobtrusively in the background. Café Beaubourg is a must, if only to experience the vibrant atmosphere.

The choice of food includes omelettes, salads, grilled steak, Chicken Cordon Bleu to mouthwatering pastries. In summer, tables are set up on the outdoor terrace – an ideal place for people-watching.

Above: Inside the café

Centre Georges Pompidou

With its startling "inside out" façade of coloured utility pipes – green for water, blue for air-conditioning and yellow for electricity – and its red translucent escalator tubes that snake up the side of the building, the Centre Georges Pompidou comes as a bit of a shock at first sight. This is especially so if you have just enjoyed a leisurely walk around the elegant 18th-century mansions of the Marais district.

Controversial through and through, the centre attracted scathing criticism when the plans of Richard Rogers and Renzo Piano were unveiled and construction started in 1971 and the centre still has its share of critics. Named after the then president of France, Georges Pompidou, and part of a programme to give Paris a facelift, the ultra-modern, high-tech centre opened to the

Above: The futuristic design includes translucent spaces, pipes and scaffolding

79 B2

Centre Georges Pompidou
place Georges Pompidou

01 44 78 12 33

www.centrepompidou.fr

Wed–Mon 11–10

Moderate to expensive

Rambuteau, Hôtel de Ville

Left: The Pompidou's cavernous interior houses a huge variety of art exhibits
Above: A viewing deck high above the place Georges Pompidou

public in 1977. A popular attraction in the city, it is affectionately called the Beaubourg Centre, after the area in which it stands.

One of the main cross-cultural institutions of the city, the complex houses the modern art museum, the Musée National d'Art Moderne, on the fourth and fifth floors, where you can view around 50,000 artworks from 1905 to the present day – including works of cubism by Georges Braque and pop art by the one and only Andy Warhol.

Other collections showcase fauvism, surrealism and abstract expressionism,

Design, with its focus on 20th-century architecture. Temporary exhibitions are regularly held here. In addition, a massive library and resource centre on levels one, two and three attracts students from all over the world, and there are bookshops, a post office, a cinema, and even a children's workshop that is immensely popular.

For an atmospheric place to eat, try the restaurant Georges on the top floor and, of course, you cannot leave the centre without a ride on an external, translucent escalator – one of the building's most striking features – for a great view of the city and the bustling piazza below.

Street performers, such as jugglers and mime artists, mingle with painters and roller-skaters in the place Georges Pompidou, a piazza directly in front of the museum.

plus a section devoted to the works of the Russian artist Kandinsky, French master Matisse, and the Spanish greats Joan Miró and Picasso. Look out for Brancusi's Studio, an area devoted to the Romanian sculptor Constantin Brancusi that has an extensive collection of his abstract works.

The Centre Georges Pompidou also houses the Bibliothèque Publique d'Information and the Centre of Industrial

Above: The Stravinsky fountain near the Centre Pompidou
Below: The piazza separates elegant Parisian houses from the futuristic centre

Église Saint-Eustache

One of the largest medieval churches of Paris, Saint-Eustache displays strong Renaissance influences. The combination gives it an authoritative look. Work first started on the church around 1532, but funds were scarce and René Benoist, the priest of the Église Saint-Eustache, sought donations to complete its construction. Several pillars of the nave and windows were added, yet the church remains unfinished to this day.

At one time it was regarded as a royal church because of its size and proximity to the then palace of the Louvre. King Louis XIV was baptised here. Other notable events include the burial of Jean-Baptiste Colbert, a leading 17th-century figure, and also that of the renowned music theorist Jean-Phillip Rameau. Simon Arnauld de Pomponne, Secretary of State for Foreign Affairs under Louis XIV, was married in this church.

Today, the main attraction is the fine organ with 8,000 pipes, one of the largest in the country.

Left: Église Saint-Eustache marks the beginning of the Les Halles area

✚ **79 A1**

✉ **Église Saint-Eustache**
rue Rambuteau

☎ 01 42 36 31 05

🕐 Daily 9:30–7

✋ Free

Ⓜ Les Halles

Église Saint-Merri

Dedicated to Saint-Merri, the 8th-century Abbot of Autun Abbey, Medericus, who is the patron saint of the Right Bank, this small church stands proudly and defiantly just off the bustling rue Saint Martin. While it dates from 1500, construction was not completed until 1612. Flamboyantly Gothic in style, its perpendicular character also displays strong English influences.

Among the things to see here are the Renaissance stained-glass windows, especially those around the nave, the 18th-century pulpit, and an organ reconstructed in 1781 by Cliquot, the famous organ builder. The well-known composer Camille Saint-Saëns is said to have played on this organ. Today, regular organ recitals are held in Église Saint-Merri.

The church houses the oldest bell in Paris, cast in 1331 and one of the few that survived the French Revolution. The pretty church is a popular sightseeing stop for tourists.

Right: Place Igor Stravinsky and the Église Saint-Merri

 79 B2

✉ **Église Saint-Merri**
76 rue de la Verrerie

☎ 01 42 71 40 75

🕙 Daily

✋ Free

🚇 Hôtel de Ville

Maison Européenne de la Photographie

This centre for contemporary photography is housed in the magnificent 18th-century Hôtel Hénault de Cantobre which was converted into a massive exhibition space during the last century, to which a new wing was later added.

The centre is designed to offer easy access to the three basic media of photography, which include exhibition prints, the printed page and film. With a permanent collection of around 12,000 works – dating from 1961 to the present day – the centre displays permanent and temporary exhibits from around the world in its stylish galleries spread over five floors. The bookshop is renowned for its rare selection pertaining to photography, which visitors can access. They can also carry out their research in its well-stocked video library and research centre.

The rare works of Jean-Wolf Sieff, Martin Parr, Larry Clark and Christian Boltanski can be seen here.

Above: The Maison Européenne de la Photographie

🕂 **79 C3**

✉ **Maison Européenne de la Photographie**
5–7 rue de Fourcy

☎ 01 44 78 75 00

🌐 **www.mep-fr.org**

🕙 Wed–Sun 11–7:30

💵 Moderate

🚇 St-Paul, Pont Marie

Musée d'Art et d'Histoire du Judaïsme

Formerly scattered collections of Jewish art in the city have been brought together in this museum. Among other artefacts, it displays traditional ceremonial and religious objects from medieval to present times, and a collection of furniture and art by artists such as Modigliani and Chagall.

✚ **79 B2**

✉ **Musée d'Art et d'Histoire du Judaïsme**
71 rue du Temple

☎ 01 53 01 86 60

🆆 **www.mahj.org**

🕐 Mon–Fri 11–6,
Sun 10–6

👜 Moderate

🚇 Rambuteau,
Hôtel de Ville

The Musée d'Art et d'Histoire du Judaïsme was founded in 1988, and is the successor to the Musée d'Art Juif de Paris, which was established in 1948 by a private association to celebrate a culture all but destroyed by the Holocaust. The museum has an excellent introductory area, followed by a series of rooms with epoch, geographical and cultural themes.

Most of the exhibits are French in origin, and come from Europe and north Africa. Notable collections include those from the Musée National du Moyen Âge, a once private collection (subsequently given to the state) that was exhibited in the Universal Exhibition of 1878 and played a key role in recognising the Jewish art.

Other works are from the Musée National d'Art Moderne at the Centre Georges Pompidou, the Musée du Louvre and the Musée d'Orsay.

Above: The Musée d'Art et d'Histoire du Judaïsme is housed in in the Hôtel de Saint-Aignan

Musée des Arts et Métiers

A museum dedicated to science and technical innovation, the Musée des Arts et Métiers has an astonishing collection of over 80,000 objects, including a copy of the standard metre and Foucault's original pendulum.

The collection is owned by the Conservatoire National des Arts et Métiers, which was founded in the late 1700s to preserve scientific instruments and inventions. Housed in the former priory of Saint-Martin-des-Champs, just a short walk from the Centre Georges Pompidou, the museum is a favourite with students and teachers of science, as well as tourists keen to learn more about discoveries and inventions.

Among its other exhibits are antique navigation instruments, clocks, steam engines, optics, underwater equipment such as the diving suit, telecommunication inventions such as Morse code and telegraphs, and a host of mechanical toys and vintage cars – a fascinating place to spend some time.

Above: The former priory of Saint-Martin-des-Champs now houses a absorbing museum

✠ **79 B1**

✉ **Musée des Arts et Métiers**
60 rue Réaumur

☎ 01 53 01 82 00

🌐 **www.arts-et-metiers. net**

🕐 Tue–Sun 10–6, Thu until 9:30pm

🖐 Moderate

Ⓜ Arts et Métiers

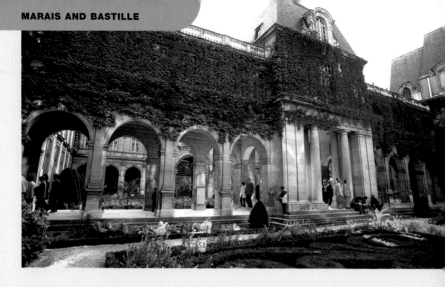

Musée Carnavalet

This museum explains everything you need to know about Paris, from its origins as a small community on the island known as Île de la Cité to the world-class metropolis it is today. It is located in two charming 17th-century townhouses, the renovated buildings of the old hotels of Carnavalet and Furrier of Saint-Fargeau, linked by a first-floor gallery.

✚ **79 D3**

✉ **Musée Carnavalet**
23 rue de Sévigné

☎ 01 44 59 58 58

🌐 **www.paris.org**

🕐 Tue–Sun 10–5:45

✋ Free; temporary exhibitions moderate

🚇 St-Paul

The courtyard of what was once the Hôtel Carnavalet serves as the entrance to the museum. A series of paintings and memorabilia that look entirely in place in the two buildings, trace the history of the city from Roman times through the Middle Ages, the Renaissance, and the extravagant reigns of Louis XIV, Louis XV and Louis XVI. Next door, the exhibits focus on the Revolution and the changes in the city under Napoleon I and Napoleon III, the Second Empire and the belle époque era.

The 20th century is depicted in the final part of the museum. Exhibits here have reconstructed interiors and paintings by Maurice Utrillo and Paul Signac.

The building is as interesting as its contents. The interiors are entirely original, featuring lavishly painted and sculpted ceilings and walls. Other *objets d'art* and documents enhance the ambience and the whole visitor experience.

Above: Ivy covers the front of the Musée Carnavalet

MAIRIE DE PARIS

HÔTEL DE DONON
(XVIe-XVIIe SIÈCLE
COLLECTIONS D'ART
DU XVIIIe SIÈCLE LÉ
À LA VILLE DE PARIS

Musée Cognacq-Jay

PAR ERNEST COGNAC
(1839-1928)
VISITES DU MARDI
AU DIMANCHE
DE 10H À 17H40

Musée Cognacq-Jay

It may be one of the lesser known museums in Paris, but this fascinating place offers a truly unique and personal view of the fashionable Parisian social set of the early 1900s. The Musée Cognacq-Jay is the result of a remarkable collection of memorabilia amassed by couple-about-town Ernest Cognacq and his wife Marie-Louise Jay.

Founders of the shop La Samaritaine, the couple were keen collectors of European art and counted among the city's wealthiest residents. Their personal collection of mainly 18th-century paintings by artists such as Lemoyne Chardin, Canaletto, Fragonard, Greuze, Tiepolo and Rembrandt, along with decorative *objets d'art*, furniture and sculptures collected from around 1900 to 1925, make for an enchanting display.

The collection is housed in a wonderful 18th-century mansion with richly carved wood-panelled rooms, not very far from the Musée Carnavalet, in what was the most fashionable residential area when the Cognacqs were alive.

Above: The Musée Cognacq-Jay houses a collection of 18th-century art in the renovated Hôtel Donon

✚ **79 C3**

✉ **Musée Cognacq-Jay**
Hôtel Donon, 8 rue Elizévir

☎ 01 40 27 07 21

🖳 **www.cognacq-jay. paris.fr**

🕐 Tue–Sun 10–6

♿ Free

Ⓜ St-Paul, Chemin-Vert

Musée Picasso

When Picasso, the great 20th-century artist, died in 1973, his vast private collection of works was donated to France by his family, largely in lieu of massive inheritance tax bills. This museum was subsequently created by the state in his memory.

An overwhelming collection of paintings, sculptures, drawings, engravings and ceramics created by the artist is on display in this renovated 17th-century mansion, the Hôtel Salé, in the heart of historic Paris. The museum tells the story of how Picasso, who was born in 1881 and began studying art some 14 years later, learned and developed his skills.

The choice of the elegant Hôtel Salé as the location for the museum, considered to be one of the finest houses in the Marais, was the subject of some debate after a competition was held to find a suitable place to display Picasso's modernistic work. Roland Simounet's inspired combination of the elegant interior of the building with modern display techniques emerged the winner. The mansion has since been restored by Bernard Vitry and Bernard

Fonquernie of the Monuments Historiques organisation between 1974 and 1980, and again in 1985.

The museum contains documents and photographs relating to Picasso's life, in addition to his own artistic output, and private collection. Picasso favoured contemporaries such as the post-Impressionist Paul Cézanne and Henri Matisse, whose paintings he bought to add to his collection. Matisse also owned works by Degas, Rousseau, Seurat and de Chirico.

A second-floor area houses temporary exhibitions and there is a library on the third floor. This a fascinating stop on any art-lover's sightseeing agenda.

Left: The museum's grand interior
Below: A sculptural detail of the 17th-century Hôtel Salé exterior

✠ **79 C2**

✉ **Musée Picasso**
   Hôtel Salé, 5 rue de Thorigny

☎ 01 42 71 25 21

🌐 **www.musee-picasso.fr**

🕐 Wed–Mon 9:30–6
   (Apr–Sep until later)

✋ Expensive

Ⓜ St-Paul, St-Sebastien Froissard

Pavillon de l'Arsenal

This may not appeal to every visitor to Paris, but the Pavillon de l'Arsenal is without doubt a fascinating place to spend a few hours if architecture and town planning are your passion. With carefully devised and well-presented exhibits, the venue showcases the history of urban Paris, and explains how the city's architecture has evolved over the years.

79 C4

Pavillon de l'Arsenal
21 boulevard Morland

01 42 76 33 97

www.pavillon-arsenal.com

Tue–Sat 10:30–6:30, Sun 11–7

Sully-Morland

Scale models, drawings, photographs, newspaper clippings and documents housed over three floors, as well as a gallery dedicated to temporary exhibitions, keep this centre at the forefront of educating visitors on the development of the city. Guides are available in several languages, and workshops make this a popular destination for budding and experienced architects.

The centre lies just a short walk from the Port Sully boulevard Henri IV near the Île Saint-Louis, and has its own bookshop with an especially good selection on Paris.

Above: Entrance to the Pavillon de l'Arsenal

Place des Vosges

One of the most engaging squares in the area, connecting the Marais with Bastille, the place des Vosges has rows of elegant, linked town houses with steep-pitched roofs and formal gardens, many with arcaded façades commissioned by Henri IV. It could be viewed as the first example of town planning in Paris.

The king also had two royal pavilions positioned at the north and south ends and declared it the place Royale. It was re-named in recognition of the département of the Vosges, in southeast France, being the first French district to pay taxes after the Revolution.

The square was unveiled in 1612 with much fanfare. It was previously the site of a royal palace, the Hôtel des Tournelles, built in 1388, which later fell out of favour and was deliberately destroyed by Catherine de Médicis in 1559.

Since then, famous Parisians have chosen to live in the square. Victor Hugo, whose house is now a museum, lived here. Smart shops, restaurants and art galleries add to its ambience.

Above: The place des Vosges is considered Paris' best preserved square

✚ **79 D3**

✉ **Place des Vosges**
3rd/4th arrondissement

🌐 **www.paris.org/
monuments**

🚇 Bastille, Chemin Vert

Rue des Rosiers

A lively street of synagogues, kosher butchers and restaurants, fast-food shops selling *falafel* (a fried delicacy made from spiced fava beans served in pitta bread), Jewish sweet shops and Hebrew bookshops, the rue des Rosiers is a heady mix of orthodox Jewish community life.

Throughout Paris there are Jewish communities, but most fled to the rue des Rosiers in the Marais – which then lay outside the boundary of the city – when they were expelled from the centre some 600 years ago. Periods of turbulence have befallen the community over the centuries, most notably during World War II when many of its residents, including children, were taken to prison camps.

Today, the street is known for its glittering array of minimalist fashion houses. The house at No 10 is a particularly good example of art nouveau architecture.

✚ 79 C3

✉ Rue des Rosiers

Ⓜ St-Paul

Above: A collection of traditional sweets on display in a shop in the rue des Rosiers

Rue Vieille-du-Temple

This is the main street that runs through the centre of trendy Marais. It has stores selling the latest in European fashion, chic hairdressing salons, art galleries, jewellery shops and shoemakers, and lively wine bars and restaurants in historic houses full of character.

Dating from 1270, this 85m (279-foot) street takes its name from a time when the Templars would walk its length to a temple that lay at one end.

Over the years rue Vieille-du-Temple has been known as the street of the Culture of the Temple, street of the Barbette Door, Barbette Street and Old Barbette Street. Among its most notable buildings are the Hôtel de Vibraye or Schomberg at No 15, dating from 1650 and restored in 1980, and the Hôtel Amelot de Bisseuil, known as the Ambassadors of Holland, built between 1657 and 1660 at No 47.

Above: Interior of the Fiesta Galerie furnishing shop in rue Vieille-du-Temple

✚ **79 C2**

✉ **Rue Vieille-du-Temple**

Ⓜ St-Paul

Louvre and Champs-Élysées

With the Arc de Triomphe towering at the head of the Champs-Élysées, and the world's leading museum, the Musée du Louvre, in a direct line of vision past the place de la Concorde towards the east, this area of Paris a magnet for the millions who visit the city every year. It is also one of the finest residential areas of the city.

LOUVRE AND CHAMPS-ÉLYSÉES WALK

1. Place de la Concorde
See page 122

Once the centre of the French Revolution and the site of the infamous guillotine that beheaded royals, including Marie Antoinette, the place de la Concorde is today a grand open space with elegant buildings and street furniture. In its central island is a 3,000-year-old Egyptian obelisk. To the east of the square is the Jardin des Tuileries.

2. Jardin des Tuileries
See page 111

There is nothing quite like a stroll through the Jardin des Tuileries on a Sunday morning. From the gardens you can see the Louvre in one direction in a straight line with the Arc de Triomphe along the Champs-Élysées. From here, exit the gardens under the Carrousel arch towards the Musée du Louvre.

3. Musée du Louvre
See page 114

With around 35,000 exhibits on display and many more in storage, the Musée du Louvre is the world's largest museum. Its grand architecture is in stark contrast to the modernist glass pyramid entrance. From here, walk under one of the arches that lead to the rue de Rivoli, turn right into avenue de l'Opéra and head to the place de l'Opéra.

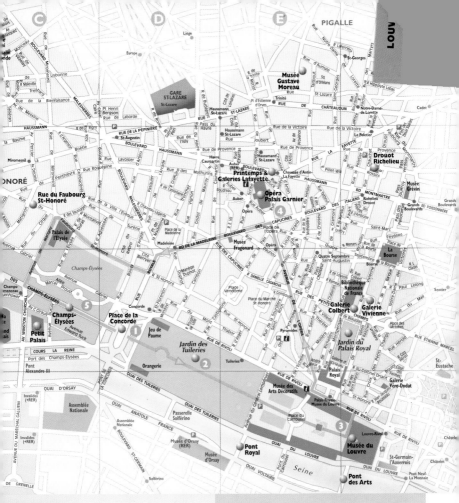

PIGALLE

Musée Gustave Moreau

GARE ST-LAZARE

Printemps & Galeries Lafayette

Drouot Richelieu

Musée Grévin

Rue du Faubourg St-Honoré

Opéra Palais Garnier

Palais de l'Élysée

Musée Fragonard

La Bourse

Champs-Élysées

Place Vendôme

Bibliothèque Nationale de France

Champs-Élysées

Place de la Concorde

Petit Palais

Jeu de Paume

Galerie Colbert

Galerie Vivienne

Jardin des Tuileries

Jardin du Palais Royal

Orangerie

Galerie Véro-Dodat

Assemblée Nationale

Musée des Arts Décoratifs

Palais-Royal Musée du Louvre

Musée d'Orsay

Pont Royal

Musée du Louvre

St-Germain-l'Auxerrois

Pont des Arts

Seine

---

4. Opéra Palais Garnier
See page 118

The Opéra Palais Garnier was built by Napoleon III to Charles Garnier's grandiose design. From place de l'Opéra head west along boulevard des Capucines, into boulevard de la Madeline and left into rue Royale. Then turn right along rue du Faubourg St-Honoré and left into the avenue de Marigny to the Champs-Élysées.

5. Champs-Élysées
See page 106

With its trees, smart shops and street cafés, where Parisians and visitors alike sit and watch the world go by, the avenue is one of the most famous in Paris, if not the world. At one end, the Arc de Triomphe stands majestically at the Charles de Gaulle-Étoile, while at the other is the place de la Concorde where our walk of this area ends.

PLACE
CHARLES DE GAULLE

Arc de Triomphe

The Arc de Triomphe stands majestically in the centre of the Étoile, a large roundabout designed by Baron Haussmann, from which 12 avenues, including the Champs-Élysées, emanate. It is celebrated as one of the greatest – if not *the* greatest – triumphal arches in the world.

The arch was commissioned by Napoleon to commemorate his victorious battles. He had already built an arch at the place du Carrousel, but was disappointed with its final size and went on to supercede it with the much larger and grander Arc de Triomphe. Work on the 50m (164-foot) tall structure began in 1806, but was not completed until 30 years later under Louis-Phillippe, largely because of Napoleon's defeat and fall from power. Fittingly, his funeral procession passed under the arch on its way to its final resting place at Les Invalides.

✚ **100 A2**

✉ **Arc de Triomphe**
place Charles-de-Gaulle

☎ 01 55 37 73 77

🌐 **www.monuments-nationaux.fr**

🕐 Apr–Sep, daily 10am–11pm;
Oct–Mar, 10am–10:30pm

✋ Moderate

Ⓜ Charles de Gaulle-Étoile

Left: The Arc de Triomphe was commissioned by Napoleon as a victory memorial
Above: A detail of the arch's ceiling

Left: The Champs-Élysées, as seen from the top of the 50m (164-foot) high Arc de Triomphe. The 2km (1.2-mile) long Champs-Élysées dates back to 1616 when Marie de Médicis turned the area into a fashionable driveway

Today, the arch remains a symbol of pride and regularly hosts national commemorations. On 8 May each year it plays a central role in the VE Day celebrations; on 14 July it hosts an event to mark Bastille Day; and Napoleon's victory at the Battle of Austerlitz in 1805 is marked at the foot of the arch on 2 December. Beneath the arch is the Tomb of the Unknown Soldier, a victim of World War I, who was buried on 11 November 1920, and where Remembrance Day events are held every year. A Memorial Flame above the tomb is lit at 6:30pm every day.

The arch is lavishly adorned with sculptures by Jean-Pierre Cortot, Antoine Étex and François Rude. Among them is Rude's famous liberty sculpture, *La Marseillaise*. Above the sculptures is a frieze depicting Napoleon's troops leaving for battle and their victorious return, along with 30 shields, each of which bears the name of a revolutionary or Imperial victory. Cortot's relief depicts the Treaty of Vienna peace agreement of 1810, while others portray the

Battle of Aboukir by Seurre the Elder and the Battle of Austerlitz by Gechter. General Marceau's funeral is shown in a bas-relief above the entrance to the arch's museum.

Crowning the Arc de Triomphe is a viewing platform from where you can see Haussmann's design of 12 avenues and the world-renowned axis, or line of vision, known as the Axe Historique. This runs from the Grande Arche at La Défense to the Arc de Triomphe, along the Champs-Élysées to the obelisk in the centre of the place de la Concorde, and on to the Arc de Triomphe du Carrousel and the Musée du Louvre. Placed in a perfect straight line, they constitute a grand panorama.

Inside the arch is a museum that tells the fascinating history of the structure, and details of Napoleon's victories. If you feel energetic enough, you can walk up the 284 steps to the viewing platform.

Above: The scale of the Arc de Triomphe appropriately expresses its purpose as a monument to victory
Below: Viewing Paris from the top of the Arc de Triomphe

Champs-Élysées

The Champs-Élysées is listed among the most famous thoroughfares in the world. This elegant avenue is 2km (1.2 mile) long and links the Arc de Triomphe at the place Charles de Gaulle to the place de la Concorde. The upper part of the avenue has offices, cafés, theatres, restaurants – most notably Fouquet's – and shops, while the lower part is bordered by chestnut trees, flower beds and grand buildings, such as the Grand Palais and Petit Palais.

The area was originally full of fields and the avenue was created when Marie de Médicis decided to extend the gardens of the Palais des Tuileries. The royal gardener, André Le Nôtre, was instructed to plant an arbour of trees, known as the Grand Cours (the Great Way). Later, it was designated the Champs Élysées, or the Elysian Fields, and began appearing on maps as an avenue from around the mid- to late 18th century. It soon became fashionable and grand houses began to be built along its length, followed by graceful fountains, statues, elegant street furniture and cafés.

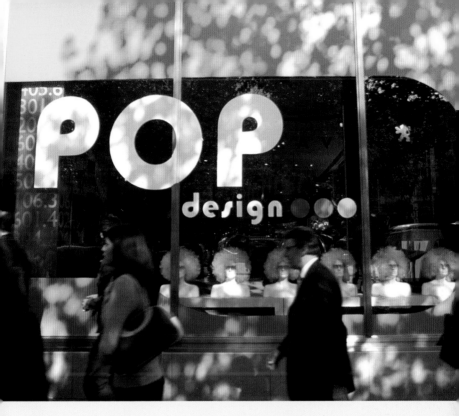

Today, the avenue is the scene of many celebrations, state processions and victory parades, most notably those for Bastille Day, when the largest military parade in Europe marches the length of the Champs-Élysées. The avenue is also gloriously lit at Christmas and New Year when it becomes a venue for parties. Traditionally, it is the last stage of the famous Tour de France cycle race.

✚ **101 C3**

✉ **Avenue des Champs-Élysées**

🕐 24 hours

✋ Free

🚇 Champs-Élysées, Clemenceau

Above left: Pedestrians walk down the world-famous Champs-Élysées
Above: The grandeur of the architecture is broken up by fun, modern shopfront designs

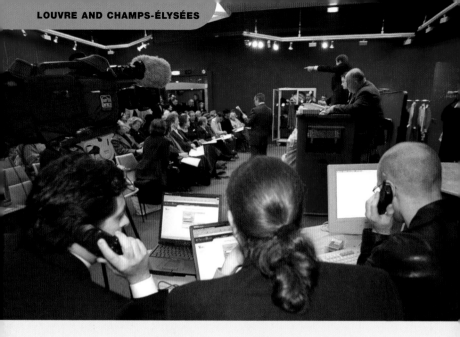

Drouot Richelieu

Everything from antique furniture from the classic French period, *objets d'art* from around the world, elaborate clocks and pendulums to jewellery, rare books and paintings, some of them by known artists, and even cars and commercial vehicles, can go under the hammer at this fashionable auction house near the Opéra Palais Garnier.

➕ **101 F2**

✉ **Drouot Richelieu**
9 rue Drouot

☎ 01 48 00 20 20

🌐 **www.gazette.drouot.com**

🕐 Mon–Sat 11–6; auctions start at 2pm

✋ Free

Ⓜ Richelieu-Drouot

Housed in a huge historic building in the rue Drouot, the auction house is open for viewing before auctions and on certain days collectors, and others can browse and examine the wide and eclectic range of items for sale. Auctions are held in various rooms throughout the building, with several different themed events held at the same time. It is worth a visit to experience the hustle and bustle, and the speed with which items are sold, even though many purchases are planned in advance. Drouot Richelieu is in the same league as Sotheby's and Christie's and transacts more business than any other auction house in Paris. It is interesting to watch the auctions, even if you are not planning to buy anything.

Above: Auction time at the Drouot Richelieu

Galeries Vivienne and Colbert

With its labyrinths of 19th-century alleyways, classic architecture, arched glass roof and original mosaic floors, the Galerie Vivienne and Galerie Colbert are among the gems of Paris, one of the earliest forms of shopping mall, where the rich would shop for exquisite items of clothing, collectables and various household goods, displayed along the 140 covered passageways that once formed the complex.

There are fewer passageways today, but of those that are left most house fine wine shops, bookshops, art shops, fashionable cafés and designer clothes, such as in Jean Paul Gaultier's exclusive showroom.

Many of the original buildings of Galerie Colbert (originally a car workshop and garage until 1980) are now given over to the Institut National de l'Histoire de l'Art in the University of Paris, which hosts many respected art exhibitions. The chance to sip coffee, shop or admire an art collection in such historic surroundings will make a trip well worthwhile.

Above: Visitors enjoy a cup of coffee or a light snack at Galerie Vivienne

- ✝ **101 F3**
- ✉ **Galerie Colbert**
  32 rue de Penthievre
- ☎ 01 40 76 00 08
- 🌐 **www.galerie-colbert. com**
- 🕐 Mon–Fri 11–7, Sat by appointment
- ✋ Free
- 🚇 Cardinal Lemoine

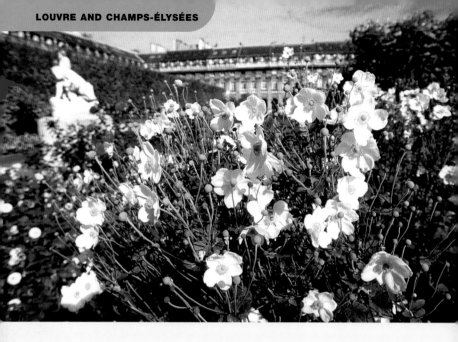

Jardin du Palais-Royal

One of the prettiest gardens in Paris, the Jardin du Palais-Royal is identified by 18th-century arcades that surround the main area of greenery and walkways. The serene garden has a collection of striped modern pillars at the Cour d'Honneur, created to the contemporary designs of Daniel Buren.

✚ **101 F3**

✉ **Jardin du Palais-Royal**
place du Palais-Royal

☎ 01 47 03 92 16

🖳 **www.monument-paris.com**

🕓 Daily 7:30am to around 10:30pm, depending on the season

🖐 Free

🚇 Palais-Royal, Musée du Louvre

The garden is flanked on both sides by shops – to the west a few old ones, and to the east more fashionable designer outlets and art galleries. To the north is a famous Parisian landmark, the old and much visited restaurant Le Grand Véfour.

A backdrop to the gardens is the classically elegant Palais Royal, home to Cardinal Richelieu (who was responsible for starting the building), Louis XIV in the 1640s, and various members of royalty.

The 18th-century palace now houses the Conseil Constitutionnel, or the State Council, along with the government department, the Ministère de la Culture. The Louvre was housed here at one time.

Above: Summer flowers bloom in the neatly landscaped gardens

Jardin des Tuileries

Strolling through the Jardin des Tuileries on any day of the week is always delightful, but on a Sunday morning it is one of the most memorable things to do while in Paris.

Dating back to 1564, when the gardens were originally created alongside the Tuileries Palace on the instructions of Catherine de Médicis, the gardens became a fashionable place for the aristocracy to parade in pre-Revolution times. They remain one of the places for people-watching today.

The gardens are around 26ha (63 acres) in size and have been remodelled over the years, most notably by André Le Nôtre in 1664, when he adopted a more formal approach to the layout. The gardens run alongside the Seine from the place de la Concorde to the Musée du Louvre, with statues, flower beds and mature trees along the way.

The Galerie Nationale du Jeu de Paume, a museum specialising in contemporary art, stands within the garden's perimiter, off the rue de Rivoli.

Above: Model yachts are sold beside the pools of the Jardin des Tuileries

---

+ **101 D3**

✉ **Jardin des Tuileries**
place de la Concorde

☎ 01 40 20 90 43

www **www.monument-paris. com**

🕐 Apr–Sep, daily 7:30am–10:30pm; Oct–Mar, 7:30–7:30

💶 Free

Ⓜ Tuileries, Concorde

Musée Gustave Moreau

An interesting little museum that gives the visitor an idea of how Parisian painters of the 19th century might have lived, the Musée Gustave Moreau takes its name from the Symbolist painter, who once worked in a studio on the lower floors.

✚ **101 E1**

✉ **Musée Gustave Moreau**
14 rue de la Rochefoucauld

☎ 01 48 74 38 50

🌐 **www.musee-moreau.fr**

🕐 Wed–Mon 10–12:45, 2–5:15

✋ Inexpensive; free on first Sun of the month

Ⓜ Trinité

Gustave Moreau was the teacher of Henri Matisse and a celebrated painter in his own right during the late 1800s. The museum may be in a dingy town house, but its curators have cleverly recreated the upstairs of the building to resemble an apartment in the style of Moreau's times. Items of furniture, houseware, works of art and other bric-a-brac that he is said to have favoured are displayed in

such a way that the visitor could easily imagine that the artist had laid all of the items out himself.

Among the paintings are works by Edgar Degas. Most interesting and intriguing are the depictions of dying youths on the one hand, and luscious women on the other.

Above: The walls of the re-created bedroom of Moreau's house-museum are covered with his works

Musée Jacquemart-André

Nearly 150 works by Van Dyck, Bellini, Botticelli and Rembrandt, which once belonged to avid art collectors, husband and wife Edouard André and Nélie Jacquemart, are among those displayed in the Musée Jacquemart-André.

The reception rooms contain priceless 18th-century works by Boucher and Jean-Honoré Fragonard, while Flemish paintings can be found in the library. To see the masters, head for the rooms on the upper floors. The museum also has some fine examples of Italian Renaissance art, including frescoes by Tiepolo.

Located within an easy walk of the Arc de Triomphe along the boulevard Haussmann, the museum is set in an elegant 19th-century mansion, and an audio guide is provided on entry which gives an insight into the lives of Edouard and Nélie, and their remarkable collection.

Above: A collection of European art is housed in this elegant 19th-century mansion

✚ **100 B1**

✉ **Musée Jacquemart-André**
158 boulevard Haussmann

☎ 01 45 62 11 59

🕐 Daily 10–6

✋ Expensive

Ⓜ St-Philippe-du-Roule

Musée du Louvre

Often described as the greatest museum in the world, and rightly so, the Musée du Louvre houses more than 35,000 works over four floors and three wings: the Sully to the east, which was designed by Claude Perrault in the 17th century as part of an extension plan; the Richelieu to the north; and the Denon to the south. Another 350,000 priceless works are stored in specially created environments to help maintain their condition.

Among the collections are French paintings from the 14th century, Oriental, Greek and Egyptian antiquities, sculptures from throughout Europe and Islamic art. Its most famous works are Leonardo da Vinci's *Mona Lisa*, dated 1503, the celebrated Hellenistic sculpture *Venus de Milo* from the 2nd century BC, and Jan Vermeer's

101 F4

✉ **Musée du Louvre**
99 rue de Rivoli

☎ 01 40 20 53 17

🖳 **www.louvre.fr**

🕐 Daily 9–6; open until 10pm Wed, Fri; closed Tue, 1 Jan, 25 Dec

👋 Moderate; free first Sun of each month; tickets for guided tours can be bought via the internet

Ⓜ Musée du Louvre, Palais-Royal

Left: Part of the Louvre's awesome collection
Above: The Louvre is a mecca for art lovers

Above left: 17th-century Frenchman Pierre Puget's sculptures in the Richelieu Wing of the Louvre
Above right: The galleries are vast enough for people to observe, sketch and walk past exhibits undisturbed by others
Left: Looking out of I M Pei's glass pyramid that stands in the courtyard of the museum and serves as the entrance to the three main underground areas

masterpiece *The Lacemaker*, painted around 1665. In all, almost 5,000 years of art are represented under one roof, from ancient to recent works.

Originally built as a castle in the 12th century by King Philippe-Auguste, Charles V, Henri II, Catherine de Médicis, Louis XIII and Louis XIV, among others, lived here. It was later remodelled to become a centre of art under François I. The remains of a keep, drawbridge, towers and dungeons of the medieval fortress still exist today under Cour Carrée. Fortunately, the museum was not damaged in the Revolution and Napoleon I added greatly to its collection as Henri IV had done before him.

In recent years the museum has undergone a transformation. Among its newer features is the glass pyramid at its entrance that evoked mixed responses when it was unveiled. Designed by I M Pei in 1989, it resembles a massive cut diamond that catches the light during the day and is illuminated at night.

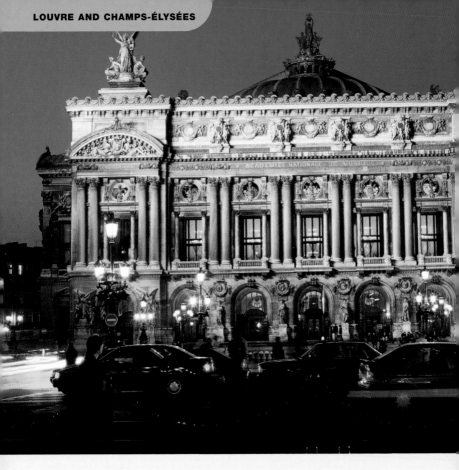

Opéra Palais Garnier

A world-class opera house, the Opéra Palais Garnier hosts international theatre, dance, musical and opera performances. This imposing building stands at the junction of the avenue de l'Opéra and the boulevard des Capucines. Rudolf Nureyev was a director of the Paris Ballet here between 1983 and 1988.

Dating from 1875 and built to the belle époque designs of Charles Garnier, the opera house has been likened to a wedding cake for its symmetrical, highly ornate gilded façade. Among its architectural features are winged horses, numerous columns and friezes, a huge sweeping staircase at its main entrance and an ornate entrance for carriages to the rear, all topped by a verdigris dome.

Inside, the foyer drips with grandeur as gilded columns, mirrors, chandeliers, balconies and murals vie for attention, while the auditorium itself is covered in gold-leaf with plush red velvet seats and an ornate false ceiling designed by Marc Chagall.

The opera house was once covered in the soot and grime of the past few decades but following a recent renovation it is now an eye-catching sight as its gold surface reflects the sunlight.

Above left: The opera house is a 'monument to art, to luxury, to pleasure'
Above: Exquisite gold statues adorn the opera house

✚ **101 E2**

✉ **Opéra Palais Garnier**
place de l'Opéra

☎ 08 92 89 90 90

🌐 **www.opera-de-paris.fr**

🕐 Daily summer 10–6; winter 10–5; closed during special events

✋ Expensive

Ⓜ Opéra

Parc de Monceau

Wedding parties are a regular sight in the Parc de Monceau, especially during the summer months, when photographs are taken beside the many follies that characterise this fun and frivolous park. It is not far from the Arc de Triomphe along the famous avenue de Wagram and boulevard de Courcelles.

✚ **100 B1**

✉ **Parc de Monceau**
boulevard de Courcelles

🕐 Apr–Oct, daily 7am–10pm;
Nov–Mar, 7am–8pm

✋ Free

🚇 Monceau

Designed in 1793 by Thomas Blaikie, who wanted to create a peaceful place to relax in the city in the style of an English garden, the park follows a classic landscaping concept, with trees, flower beds, ponds and borders. What sets it apart, however, is the many follies – from Greek temples to fake ruins of castles and palaces – at almost every turn.

Above: Parc Monceau is a popular spot for Parisians wishing to get away from the hustle and bustle of city life

Petit Palais

Along with the Grand Palais, the Petit Palais stands on the Right Bank of the Seine at the point where the Pont Alexandre III begins to cross the river. Built for the World Exhibition of 1900, the two palaces are constructed in an art nouveau design with much attention given to their elaborate front façades and domed roofs. They stand in carefully manicured gardens.

The Petit Palais was renovated and reopened in 2006. It is smaller than the Grand Palais, as the name suggests, but both complement each other well, on either side of avenue Winston Churchill.

The Petit Palais, like its big sister, is used as an exhibition hall and regularly hosts art and sculpture events, with works by some of the world's leading artists, along with art festivals and special events. Its static collection includes Poussin's *The Massacre of the Innocents*, Rubens' *Prosperpina* and Rembrandt's *Self-Portrait with Poodle*.

Above: The Petit Palais houses a museum collection of 19th-century French art in a lovely setting

🕂 **101 C3**

✉ **Petit Palais**
avenue Winston Churchill

☎ 01 42 65 12 73

🌐 **www.petitpalais.paris.fr**

🕐 Tue–Sun 10–5:30; phone for special exhibitions

✋ Free for permanent collections; fee varies for special exhibitions

🚇 Champs-Élysées-Clémenceau

Place de la Concorde

Designed by Ange-Jacques Gabriel and unveiled in 1755, the place de la Concorde stands at the opposite end of the Champs-Élysées from the Arc de Triomphe and was formerly known as the place Louis XV.

This square is probably most famous for being the site of the guillotine during the French Revolution in the late 1700s, when it was called place de la Révolution. King Louis XVI, Queen Marie Antoinette and Madame du Barry, the mistress of King Louis XV, were among those executed here.

It was renamed place de la Concorde in 1795, and its impressive buildings are now ranked the best of their period. To the north are two fine stone buildings housing

the Hôtel de Crillon and government offices, fountains and the Obelisk of Luxor, inscribed with hieroglyphics detailing the reign of the pharaoh Ramesses II.

A gift of the viceroy of Egypt, Mehemet Ali, in 1829, the 3,000-year-old obelisk is said to weigh over 250 tonnes and once stood at the entrance to Luxor Temple. It was brought to the place de la Concorde under the orders of King Louis-Philippe in 1833. Engravings detail the special

machinery and manoeuvres that were used to transport and position it. It marks the spot where the guillotine stood.

To the east of the place de la Concorde is the Jardin des Tuileries, with the Galerie Nationale du Jeu de Paume, a museum of contemporary art, and the Musée de l'Orangerie in view, while to the west is the Champs-Élysées and to the northeast the rue de Rivoli.

The River Seine lies along the southern side of this rectangular-shaped square, where the 18th-century Pont de la Concorde crosses to the Left Bank. Each corner of the square has statues that represent the well-known French cities of Lille, Strasbourg, Lyon, Marseille, Bordeaux, Nantes, Brest and Rouen.

Above: Ornate fountains and hieroglyphs on the ancient Luxor obelisk in the place de la Concorde

✚ **101 D3**

✉ **Place de la Concorde**

🕐 24 hours

✋ Free

Ⓜ Concorde

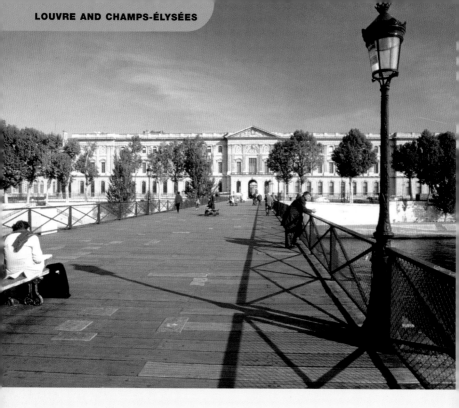

Pont des Arts

The original bridge that spanned the Seine was built in 1804 and was one of the first pedestrian iron bridges in Paris. After years of wear and tear, it was rebuilt in 1984 without any major alteration to the original design, though the number of steel arches was reduced from nine to seven.

✚ **101 F4**

✉ **Pont des Arts**

◷ 24 hours

🚇 Louvre-Rivoli

The Pont des Arts, also known as the Passerelles des Arts, has a sturdy walkway and benches that catch the evening sun.

The bridge links the Musée du Louvre's Cour Carré with the Institut de France, and is a popular spot for street performers.

It is perhaps the most romantic bridge in Paris and has a beautiful view of the Île de la Cité, one of the two islands in the Seine.

Above: Pedestrians stop to admire the view as they cross the Pont des Arts

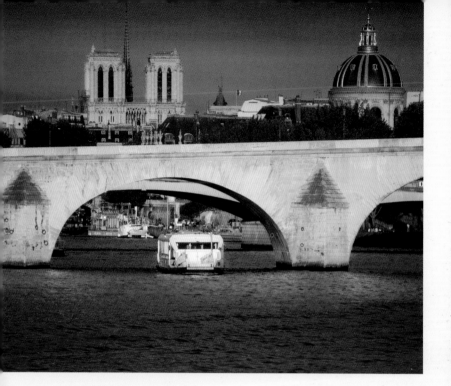

Pont Royal

One of the most classically constructed bridges in Paris, the Pont Royal belongs to the *grand siècle* when the extravagant King Louis XIV built palatial homes, innumerable squares, theatres and other structures. The Pont Royal crosses the Seine, linking the Jardin des Tuileries and the Musée du Louvre on the Right Bank with the Musée d'Orsay on the Left Bank.

The original wooden bridge was destroyed in a fire and replaced with a stone structure in 1689. Key festivals were held on this bridge in the 18th century.

Its location means it is often the scene of festivities and fireworks, and is frequented by photographers.

Take a walk on the bridge for a stunning view of the Louvre, the towers of Notre-Dame and the tip of the Tour Eiffel as well as other familiar Paris landmarks.

Above: A spectacular view from the Pont Royal of some of Paris' historic buildings

✚ **101 E4**

✉ **Pont Royal**

🕓 24 hours

🚇 Palais-Royal, Musée du Louvre

Printemps and Galeries Lafayette

The lavish department stores of Printemps and Galeries Lafayette, two of the largest names in retail, sit side by side on the boulevard Haussmann near the Opéra Palais Garnier and stock a seemingly endless selection of fine goods.

Printemps occupies three buildings, in total comprising

101 E2

✉ **Printemps and Galeries Lafayette**
64 boulevard Haussmann;
40 boulevard Haussmann

☎ 01 42 82 50 00;
01 42 82 34 56

🌐 **www.printemps.com**
www.galerieslafayette.com

🕐 Mon–Wed 9:30–7;
Thu 9:30–9

Ⓜ Opéra

nearly 4,000sq m (43,055 square feet), and claims to have the world's largest beauty department. An array of fashions for women and children are displayed over eight floors in its Printemps de la Mode store, while its Printemps de l'Homme sales clothes of all styles and price ranges for the menfolk. Printemps de la Maison features an eye-catching art nouveau stained-glass cupola, as well as a wonderful collection of furniture, ornaments, fabrics and accessories for the home.

Galeries Lafayette similarly has fashions for all the family, leather goods, top quality beauty and cosmetic products, items for the home and floors of seasonal goodies, be it summer or the Christmas season.

There is also a fabulous food hall and lounge bar. The labyrinth of departments is connected by walkways, with the home section just across the street. Try to look away from the goods if only for a few minutes to admire the architecture – it is famous for its 1912 Byzantine-style glass dome. Galeries Lafayette, which opened in 1893, is, like Printemps, a Parisian institution and a visit is a must.

Above: The balconies and glass dome of the Galeries Lafayette, a chic department store packed full of high-class goods

Rue du Faubourg Saint-Honoré

Hermès, Gucci, Dolce e Gabbana and Yves Saint Laurent are just some of the major names in fashion that have discreet little shops along the rue du Faubourg Saint-Honoré, one of the most fashionable streets in the world for discerning shoppers. Take a walk here and you will soon see why Paris is known as the mecca of haute couture.

Paris, in general, is a great shopping city and Faubourg Saint-Honoré is where you will find the best of the big labels. This is the street where movie stars come, where the shops and their windows are as exquisitely created as the clothes they sell.

This long street, which takes its name from the French Saint Honorious of Amiens and stretches from the boulevard Courcelles junction to the rue de Rivoli, is also home to a number of government buildings and embassies. The British Embassy is at No 35.

Above: Macaroons in a variety of exotic flavours on sale in the Ladurée patisserie in the Faubourg Saint-Honoré

- ✚ **101 C2**
- ✉ **Rue du Faubourg Saint-Honoré**
- 🕐 Shops: Mon–Sat 9:30–7
- Ⓜ Madeleine/Miromesnil

Montmartre

Populated by cabaret entertainers, writers and artists living the bohemian life, Montmartre has remained surprisingly unchanged in character from the 19th and early 20th centuries. Its tiny streets and squares, especially the place du Tertre, where portraitists will sketch or paint a willing passer-by in minutes, attract visitors in droves, as does Pigalle, home to the famous Moulin Rouge. However, its most popular site is undoubtedly the Sacré-Coeur, perched on a hill, offering a panoramic view of this lively area.

128

A WALK AROUND MONTMARTRE

1. Cimetière de Montmartre
See page 132

The cemetery is an interesting place to spend some time. It is the final resting place of many famous names, including the artist Edgar Degas. Leave by the rue Caulaincourt exit and head down the boulevard de Clichy, past the Moulin Rouge, then turn left into rue Houdon.

2. Place des Abbesses
See page 134

This square is a good place to stop for a coffee and mix with the locals. Several buildings feature art nouveau styling, including the church of St-Jean-de-Montmartre and the métro entrance, which leads to the deepest station in Paris. Continue north from the square along rue de la Vieuville and rue Drevet to the place du Tertre.

3. Place du Tertre
See page 135

Numerous artists congregate in this centuries-old square, enjoying the praise of passing visitors as they paint. They will immortalise on canvas any visitor who cares to sit and pose for a while. The square has a number of lively coffee shops and cafés. From here make your way to the steps of the Sacré-Coeur, which is clearly signposted.

4. Sacré-Coeur
See page 136

Providing one of the finest panoramic views of the city, the Sacré-Coeur stands on the highest point in Paris. This Romanesque-Byzantine basilica honours the dead of the Franco-Prussian war of 1870. Board the funicular back down to Montmartre, or head off to rue Cortot to visit the Musée de Montmartre.

5. Musée de Montmartre
See page 133

The Montmartre area of Paris has a long and decidedly colourful past, with a justly famed nightlife. This museum, housed in a 17th-century mansion, lies just behind Montmartre's one and only vineyard. It once belonged to a member of Molière's stage troupe, and was the home of the artist Renoir.

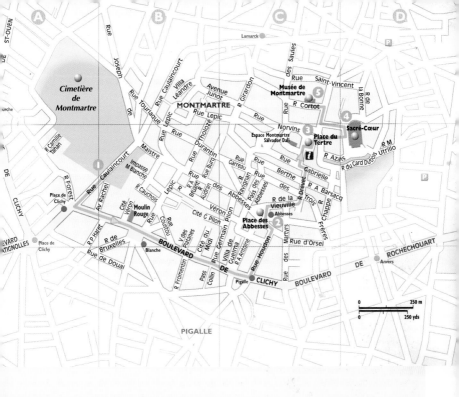

Cimetière de Montmartre

MONTMARTRE

Rue Joseph de Maistre
Rue Caulaincourt
Rue Tourlaque
Rue Lepic
Villa Léandre
Avenue Junot
Rue Girardon
Rue des Saules
Rue Saint-Vincent
Lamarck

Musée de Montmartre **5**

R Cortot

Rue Lepic
Rue Durantin
Norvins
Espace Montmartre Salvador Dali
3 Place du Tertre
Rue Norvins

4 Sacré-Cœur
R de la Bonne
R du Card Dubois Utrillo

R Camille Tainan
R Forest
Rue Caulaincourt
Av Rachel
Impasse M Blanche
R Cauchois
Cité Véron
Rue Burq
Rue Durantin
Rue Garreau
Rue Ravignan
Pass des Abbesses
Rue des Abbesses
Rue
Berthe
R A Barsacq
Rue Gabrielle
R des Trois
R Chappe
R Azas

Place de Clichy
Moulin Rouge
Cité Véron
Rue Coustou
Cité G Pilon
Véron
Rue Audran
Rue des Abbesses
R de la Vieuville
2 Place des Abbesses
Abbesses

DE CLICHY
Place de Clichy
R P Haret
R de Bruxelles
Rue de Douai
Blanche
BOULEVARD DE CLICHY
V des Platines
Cité du Midi
Cité de Guelma
R A Antoine
Pass Collin
R Fromentin
Rue Houdon
Pigalle
Rue des Martyrs
Rue d'Orsel

DE ROCHECHOUART
Anvers
BOULEVARD

BOULEVARD DES BATIGNOLLES

PIGALLE

DE ST-OUEN

0 ___ 250 m
0 ___ 250 yds

Cimetière de Montmartre

Under the highly ornate tombs of the Montmartre cemetery lie the district's famous former residents. A walk will reveal the graves of many familiar names – writers, artists, musicians and others.

✚ **131 A1**

✉ **Cimetière de Montmartre**
avenue Rachel

☎ 01 53 42 36 30

🕐 Daily 8–6

♿ Free

Ⓜ Clichy/Blanche

Here you can seek out the final resting place of the writers Alexandre Dumas and Henri Stendhal, the Russian dancer Nijinsky, artist Edgar Degas, composers Hector Berlioz and Jacques Offenbach, and film-maker François Truffaut. Émile Zola's tomb makes an imposing sight near the entrance, although the writer's remains are actually in the Panthéon.

The cemetery may not be an obvious choice as a place to visit, and being on a busy road below street level, may be a further deterrant, but once inside it is surprisingly peaceful. Mature trees and planted areas add to the sense of serenity. A series of organised walks and routes are suggested, with the details posted near the entrance gate.

Above: The Cimetière de Montmartre, resting place of the novelist Zola, the composer Berlioz and the painter Degas

Musée de Montmartre

Located in one of Montmartre's finest houses, this 17th-century mansion belonged to Rose de Rosimond, a member of the dramatist Molière's stage troupe. It is said that the actor died on stage in true show business style. The museum tells the captivating story of Montmartre, warts and all.

Exhibits cover the period from the 12th century, when the district had an important convent, too the present day. Along the way you can explore its wine-making days, its artistic and theatrical history and its infamous nightlife, and learn about the building of the great Sacré-Coeur.

Through a series of paintings, drawings, photographs, scale models, posters, documents and memorabilia, it recalls the time when the likes of Picasso, Toulouse-Lautrec, Renoir, Utrillo and Suzanne Valadon would sit near the mansion and paint the pictures that would become world famous. Indeed, there was a time when many of these bohemian figures lived and worked in the house.

Be sure to visit the re-created 19th-century bistro and the glorious gardens set just behind Montmartre's last remaining vineyard.

Above: The modest entrance to the Musée de Montmartre

🕇 **131 C1**

✉ **Musée de Montmartre**
12 rue Cortot

☎ 01 46 06 61 11

🌐 **www.museedemontmartre.fr**

🕐 Tue–Sun 10–6

✋ Moderate

🚇 Anvers, Lamarck-Caulaincourt

Place des Abbesses

After the din of the neighbouring place du Tertre, the tranquil place des Abbesses is the ideal place to pause, enjoy a coffee and take in the absorbing atmosphere of the area. One of Montmartre's prettiest squares, it is just a short walk from the Sacré-Coeur and Pigalle, and is a favoured Sunday morning haunt of local residents as well as visitors.

Surrounding the square are some fine examples of extravagant art nouveau architecture, the most notable of which is the canopied métro entrance that leads to Paris' deepest station at 40m (131 feet). Designed by Hector Guimard, it features amber lanterns and green wrought-iron arches, and is one of the last remaining examples in the city. The Église St-Jean-de-Montmartre, which dates from 1904, is named after the abbey that once stood on the site. The decorative windows, which significantly brighten up its otherwise austere façade, date from the same period.

✚ 131 C2

🕐 24 hours

✋ Free

🚇 Abbesses

Above: The art nouveau entrance to the city's métro system at place des Abbesses

134

Place du Tertre

This is where caricaturists, portraitists and landscape artists congregate each day to paint local scenes and willing passers-by. Visitors throng these "street studios" so that they can can take home a drawing or painting of themselves. The place du Tertre is a fascinating, though touristy, reminder of a time when Picasso or Renoir may have sat in this very square and painted.

Montmartre's oldest "village" square is also the highest point in the city at 130m (426 feet) and affords visitors a stunning view of the skyline. The narrow streets are lined with colourful restaurants, including many historic ones.

For those interested in architecture, there are some fine examples of 18th- to 20th-century houses, where the area's working-class residents once lived.

While in this area visit the Espace Dalí, a surreal museum with more than 300 works by the artist and sculptor Salvador Dalí.

Above: Artists and cafés abound in the place du Tertre

- 🕀 **131 C2**
- 🕐 24 hours
- ✋ Free
- 🚇 Anvers, Lamarck-Caulaincourt

Sacré-Coeur

The snowy white façade of the basilica set on the historic hill (the Butte) of Montmartre, nearly 130m (426 feet) above sea level, dominates the Paris skyline. The basilica is approached by a series of steep steps through narrow winding streets. However, a breathtaking view of the city makes the climb worthwhile.

Montmartre (Mount of Martyrs) is the place that marks the martyrdom of Saint Denis, the 3rd-century bishop of Paris. Legend has it that Bishop Denis picked up his severed head and carried it to the north, where the city of Saint Denis stands today.

The basilica's name means Sacred Heart and it was built in honour of the 58,000 who perished during the Franco-Prussian War (1870–71). Priests in relay still maintain the tradition of perpetual prayer for the dead. They say that nuns from the abbey which stood on the site of the Sacré-Coeur were sent to the guillotine during the French Revolution from here.

Sacré-Coeur is in stark contrast to the other Gothic and medieval religious buildings in Paris, such as Notre-Dame

or the Église Saint-Séverin. Work on the structure began in 1875 to the neo-Romanesque-Byzantine plans of architect Paul Abadie, who won a competition to find the best design. It is said to have been inspired by St Sophia's in Constantinople (Istanbul) and St Mark's in Venice. Sadly, Abadie died shortly after the foundation stone was laid, and the work was continued by six other architects.

The cost of construction amounted to around 40 million francs, with much of it coming from donations. The names of donors are carved in stone on a plaque.

Above: A gargoyle on the side of the basilica of Sacré-Coeur
Above right: Taking a breather on the steps of the church

✚ **131 D2**

✉ **Sacré-Coeur**
place du Parvis du Sacré-Coeur

☎ 01 53 41 89 00

🌐 **www.sacre-coeur-montmartre. com**

🕓 Daily 6–10:30; dome 9–6; crypt noon–6

✋ Free, dome inexpensive

🚇 Abbesses, then take the funicular or steps to the top of the hill

Work on the basilica took some 38 years to complete, largely because of delays in laying the foundation in land that had seen much quarrying. Underpinning pits had to be created up to 33m (108 feet) deep, without which it would sink into the clay. Although the work was complete in 1914, it was another five years before it was consecrated because of World War I.

Built in travertine stone from Château-Landon in Seine-et-Marne, it exudes calcite, which keeps it looking white despite pollution. It has the world's heaviest bell, the 19-tonne Savoyarde bell, cast in 1895 in Annecy, and a Cavaillé organ that is one of the rarest in the world. The basilica's dome is reached by a series of steps and is officially the second-highest viewpoint after the Tour Eiffel.

Among its design features is a portico of three arches with columns on either side topped with bronze statues of Joan of Arc and King (Saint) Louis IX. Inside the basilica the 20th-century Luc Olivier Merson mosaic in the apse, entitled *Christ in Majesty*, is one of the largest mosaics in the world. Note the basilica's stained-glass windows, which were added over a period of a few years from 1903, as well as its crypt vaults.

Above: The hallowed interior of Sacré-Coeur, completed in 1914 and consecrated after World War I
Right: The church was built to honour the 58,000 who were killed during the Franco-Prussian War

Further Afield

If you wish to take a break from the city centre's hustle and bustle, head further out for some truly memorable experiences. The palace of Versaille and chateau of Fontainebleau are outstanding examples of French architecture, and they are just a short journey away. Closer still are the B₀ de Boulogne, with its numerous leisure opportunities, and Disneyland® Resort Paris for some thrilling roller-coaster rides.

Bois de Boulogne

This is where Parisians go to enjoy the great outdoors at weekends. One of the city's largest parks on the outskirts to the west of the city, the Bois de Boulogne is spread over 845ha (2,090 acres), with 22km (14 miles) of paths and 56km (35 miles) of roads. Its magnificent features include formal gardens with lakes and waterfalls, and some 150,000 trees and 300,000 bushes.

The park was created by Baron Haussmann in the reign of Napoleon III, and is said to have been inspired by London's Hyde Park. It offers a whole range of leisure opportunities – from horse racing at two racecourses to cycling and jogging, and a children's play area.

There is also a mini-golf course, a toy train and puppet shows. The park's "Explor@dome" will keep youngsters amused for hours. Within the park are theme gardens such as the Shakespeare Garden, Parc de Bagatelle, Rose Garden, Jardin d'Acclimatation, and the museums of herbs and folk art.

Although the park is open 24 hours a day, it is probably best to avoid entering it after dark as it has a shady night-time reputation.

- 24 hours
- Free
- Porte Dauphine, Porte d'Auteuil

Above: One of many pleasant tree-lined pathways for a quiet walk in the Bois de Boulogne

Chantilly

The pretty town of Chantilly, one of the leading centres for training racehorses, has its own racecourse and museum – the Musée Vivant du Cheval. The town is beautiful in its own right, but most visitors head for the enchanting Château de Chantilly when taking this trip out of Paris. One of the most attractive chateaux in the region, it stands in a park designed by the famous landscape gardener André Le Nôtre. It features parterres, water courses, an English garden and a number of pavilions.

Dating from the late 1400s, the building on the estate comprises two sections: the Grand Château, which was destroyed during the French Revolution and rebuilt in the 1870s, and the Petit Château, which dates back to 1560. The latter was the home of Anne de Montmorency, the 16th-century Marshal of France and a member of one of France's most important families.

The chateau's art gallery, the Musée Condé, is home to some of the most historic paintings in France after the Musée du Louvre in the city centre, and to a collection of 15th- and 16th-century book illustrations and hundreds of rare manuscripts.

Above: The large expanse of water in front of the chateau reflects its grand buildings, the Petit Château and the Grand Château

✉ **Chantilly**

☎ 03 44 62 62 62

🌐 **www.chateaude chantilly.com**

🕐 Apr–Nov, Wed–Mon 10–6, Dec–Mar, Mon, Wed–Fri 10:30–12:45 2–5, Sat–Sun 10:30–5

✋ Moderate

🚉 Chantilly-Gouvieux

© Disney

Disneyland® Resort Paris

With its close proximity to Paris, Disneyland® Resort Paris is a destination like no other that attracts millions of visitors every year. Old or young there is something for everyone; visitors can enjoy attractions in the open air as well as indoor shows all year round. But it is around Christmas that the Resort is transformed into a Christmas winter wonderland, complete with a festive parade and Disney Characters dressed in seasonal costumes.

The Resort has three distinct areas – the Disneyland® Park, Walt Disney Studios® Park and Disney Village®. Within the Resort, there are seven Disney Hotels each with a different theme to suit every taste and budget. On its periphery there are several Selected and Associated Hotels, a golf course, shopping mall and La Vallée Village® Outlet shopping. Disneyland® Park has five lands: Adventureland, where visitors can experience life as Indiana Jones or take a journey on a ship surrounded by pirates; Frontierland, with its wild-west theme; Fantasyland, where children can soar with Dumbo the Flying Elephant or Peter Pan; Discoveryland, with incredible intergalactic

© Disney

oyages and special effects; and Main Street USA® where every day you can see he new Disney's Once Upon a Dream Parade with some of your favourite Disney Characters.

If you are still not exhausted after some 0 or more attractions, you can watch Moteur...Action! Stunt Show Spectacular® being filmed or experience Armageddon n one of the four production zones of Walt Disney Studios® Park. While you are here, take a ride in a spinning shell on the East Australian Current in Crush's Coaster inspired by Disney Pixar's *Finding Nemo*; height restrictions apply) or drive a car through Radiator Springs on Cars Race Rally (inspired by Disney Pixar's *Cars*).

Parents and children alike have great fun here. A programme of additional shows akes place throughout the day, as well as parades and film shoots.

Above left: Sleeping Beauty's Castle
Above right: One of the Madhatter's Tea Cups in Fantasyland

✉ **Disneyland® Resort Paris**

☎ 08705 03 03 03

🌐 **www.disneylandparis.com**

🕐 Opening times vary according to season. Please check website for up-to-date times

✋ Expensive

🚉 RER line A to Marne-la-Vallée Chessy/Disneyland

Fontainebleau

The exquisite Château de Fontainebleau, birthplace of Henri III and Louis XIII, is also where Napoleon signed his deed of abdication in 1814. Equally well known is the Forest of Fontainebleau, where French kings have hunted for centuries.

Fontainebleau is just 56km (35 miles) from Paris, and makes a great day out. The château is surrounded by a forest, and is one of the largest former royal residences, built in the 16th century on the site of a 12th-century château. Designed in the Italian Mannerist style, a first for France, it combined European-style painting and moulded plasterwork with metalwork, stucco and woodwork. This style came to be known as the "Fontainebleau style" and became fashionable in Paris.

The château's splendid interiors include the Galerie François I, decorated with frescoes, and the Salle de Bal – the magnificent ballroom. Many visitors come especially to see the private apartments of Emperor Napoleon and Josephine.

Over the years, 34 monarchs – including François I – successively resided in the château. Within 300 years of its construction, however, the building had fallen into disrepair and many of the original furnishings were sold during the French

Revolution to raise funds. At around this time, the town became known as Fontaine-la-Montagne, meaning "Fountain by the Mountain", although it reverted back to its original name a short while later.

Preferring this château to the then empty palace at Versailles, Napoleon Bonaparte began to restore the building's 1,900 rooms to his own extravagant design, and it once again became a grand home. Even today, its interiors remain the most exquisite anywhere in France.

While the château attracts around 300,000 visitors every year, nearly four times that number visit the great Forest of Fontainebleau, a former royal hunting ground and now an official national conservation park. The 20,000ha (49,400-acre) forest, now a World Heritage Site, is a glorious place to walk, cycle, rock-climb and watch wild birds and animals.

Above left: Conical-shaped trees line the entrance to the Château de Fontainebleau
Above: The François I Gallery in the château

✉ **Fontainebleau**

☎ 01 60 71 50 70

🌐 **www.chateaudefontainebleau. net**

🕐 Oct–May, daily 9:30–5; Jun–Sep 9:30–6; closed Tue and public holidays

✋ Moderate

🚉 Fontainebleau-Avon

La Grande Arche

Grande Arche de la Fraternité, to give it its full title, is one of Paris more recent landmarks and one that is almost impossible to miss. La Grande Arche was designed by Johan Otto Von Spreckelsen for the 1989 Bicentenary of the French Revolution. His proposal beat all others in an international competition to find a 20th-century version of the Arc de Triomphe that would celebrate humanity rather than military victory.

This Italian Carrara marble-and-glass structure is an almost perfect hollow cube, 108m (354 feet) wide, 110m (361 feet) tall and 112m (367 feet) deep. The magnificent building is located at La Défense, in a straight line from the Musée du Louvre, the Jardin des Tuileries, the place de la Concorde, the Champs-Élysées and the Arc de Triomphe. However, the building itself is slightly turned on its axis to break the straight line of the Axe Historique, or the historic axis that stretches from the Louvre's glass pyramid to the Esplanade du Général de Gaulle.

Go right to the top of La Grande Arche in a glass elevator for a stunning view of all these monuments.

The 35-storey building houses government offices, exhibitions, shops and a charming restaurant.

✉ **La Grande Arche**
La Défense

☎ 01 49 07 27 57

🔲 **www.grandearche.com**

🕔 Apr–Sep, daily 10–8;
Oct–Mar, 10–7

✋ Moderate

🚇 La Défense

Above: A colossal structure, La Grande Arche was part of the late 20th-century's architectural programme for Paris

Marché aux Puces de St-Ouen

One of the experiences that shouldn't be missed on any visit to France is the chance to spend a few hours on a Sunday morning in a flea market. Not just for buying antiques and memorabilia, flea markets are the place where residents congregate to discuss the week's events. They are always animated, noisy and colourful, and the Marché aux Puces de St-Ouen at the Porte de Clignancourt is no exception.

Covering an area of 9ha (27 acres), this market offers everything from jeans to household goods, but be sure to visit the area dedicated to antiques, just under the Périphérique overpass. Here, a number of small markets are linked by busy alleyways and goods of all descriptions can be found. At the Marché Serpette look out for art deco items and paintings, the Marché Biron for reproduction furniture,

the Marché Malik for ethnic goods and the Marché Vernaison for furniture. It is also possible to find antiques at bargain prices at the Marché Paul Bert or the Marché Cambo.

You must arrive early and be prepared to barter in true Faubourg style. Remember that at weekends you will be jostled by around 150,000 other souls all looking for a bargain.

Above: Shops inside the Marché aux Puces de St-Ouen

✉ **Marché aux Puces de St-Ouen**
Porte de Clignancourt

🕐 Sat–Mon 9–6

✋ Free

Ⓜ Porte de Clignancourt

Musée Marmottan Monet

One of the city's little gems, this is probably one of the least-known museums in Paris, purchased in 1882 by Jules Marmottan, and bequeathed to his son Paul, the elegant 19th-century mansion began to take on the appearance of a museum when an extensive collection of family paintings, furnishings and bronzes from the Renaissance and First Empire periods was introduced to its rooms. When he died in 1932, Paul Marmottan left the house and the collection to the Académie des Beaux-Arts.

The mansion was converted into a museum two years later, in 1934. The collection, boosted by generous donations over the years, really came into its own when it was the beneficiary of major works by the Impressionist painter Claude Monet,

donated by his son Michel Monet. Another addition was the Wildenstein collection of around 300 pages from 13th- to 16th-century manuscripts. Further donations, including works by Monet's contemporaries Berthe Morisot, Edgar Degas, Édouard Manet and Pierre-Auguste Renoir, have made the museum a repository of notable Impressionist work.

Important works of art include Monet's *Water-Lilies* series from his final years at Giverny, his *Impression – soleil levant*,

Above left and right: Rooms of the Musée Marmottan with its collection of Impressionist paintings

which gave the art movement its name, and Gauguin's famous *Bouquet de Fleurs*.

✉ **Musée Marmottan Monet**
2 rue Louis-Boilly

☎ 01 44 96 50 33

💻 **www.marmottan.com**

🕒 Tue–Sun 10–5:30

✋ Moderate

🚇 La Muette

Parc André-Citroën

Created on the site of a former Citroën factory, this park is full of surprises. It employs a modernist approach to landscaping, in which geometry is used to create distinctive gardens – a White Garden, Black Garden, six Serial Gardens and a Wild Garden. At every turn there are striking postmodern sculptures created from metal.

✉ **Parc André-Citroën**
rue Balard, rue LeBlanc

☎ 01 45 58 35 40

🕐 Mon–Fri 8am–dusk,
Sat–Sun 9am–dusk

✋ Free

Ⓜ Balard, Javel

When the Citroën factory was demolished, it was decided that the 5.6ha (14 acre) site, alongside the Seine like the Jardin des Tuileries and the Jardins du Trocadéro, would be converted into a garden.

In the 1980s Alain Provost and Gilles Clément won the landscaping competition with their outstanding modernist design. Their plan was to create gardens with four themes – artifice, architecture, movement and nature – that would provide a smooth transition from urban to rural. The central feature was a massive lawn with large glasshouse pavilions housing an Orangery and a Mediterranean garden, separated by a paved area with dancing fountains.

Today, the gardens attract thousands of visitors keen to see the futurist designs that remain fresh, despite being more than 25 years old.

Above: A waterway in the Parc André-Citroën

Parc Montsouris

Designed by Baron Haussmann and inspired by the traditional English style, the Parc Montsouris was part of a plan by Napoleon III to create major parks at the four cardinal points of the city. This one lies to the south of the city on the site where, according to legend, the giant Isoire was supposed to have confronted Guillaume d'Aquitaine.

Though the plans for the garden were devised around the mid-18th century, the work was not completed until 1878 because of the constraints posed by the site – a labyrinth of tunnels in the subsoil, the result of mining – and railway lines running through the area.

The problematic railway lines that criss-cross the park are now obscured from view by dense undergrowth, and are covered with bridges for walkers. The result is an impressive park – a favourite with nearby residents, students of the neighbouring Cité Universitaire and tourists.

The garden features copses of more than 1,400 trees, lawns, a lake with a waterfall, serpentine pathways, statues and play areas. The Paris Observatory, the reference point for the Paris meridian line dating from Napoleon I's era, borders the lake.

Above: Imposing pillars surround a pool in the Parc Montsouris

✉ **Parc Montsouris**
avenue Reille and
boulevard Jourdan

🌐 **www.monument-paris.**
com

🕐 Mon–Fri 8–dusk, Sat–Sun
9–dusk

✋ Free

🚇 RER Line B Cité
Universitaire

Parc de la Villette

With its glass domes and metal structures, the ultramodern 36ha (89-acre) Parc de la Villette is the largest park in Paris. It includes a science museum, a cinema and a number of follies. Look out for the music complex, the circus, the concert hall and an exhibition hall, where temporary events are held on a regular basis.

✉ **Parc de la Villette**
30 avenue Corentin-Cariou

☎ 01 40 05 80 00

🌐 **www.villette.com**

🕐 Tue–Sat 10–6, Sun 10–7

✋ Moderate

Ⓜ Porte de la Villette

The Parc de la Villette is located in the 19th district, a stone's throw from the Seine and Saint-Denis, on the site of an old slaughterhouse. It was designed by the Swiss architect Bernard Tschumi, who won the commission in a design competition. This was his first major work.

The notable design features include a covered walkway that runs the length of the park, linking its two most prominent components, the Cité de la Musique, a complex with studios, a museum and a concert hall, and the Cité des Sciences, a futuristic science museum. He also created 35 follies, red cube structures that house cafés and workshops for children, as well as sports areas.

What was once a hall for cattle has now been converted into an exhibition space and an auditorium.

Above: The steel sphere of La Géode houses the cinema within the Parc de la Villette

Père-Lachaise

The Père-Lachaise cemetery is about as far removed from being sombre as one can possibly get. Located on the outskirts of Paris, it is atmospheric, fascinating and historic, and at the same time provides a refreshingly restful place to walk and enjoy a few hours of solitude.

It covers 44ha (108 acres) on a hillside in the *faubourg* of Ménilmontant and has lots of little tree-lined pathways. The illustrious names of those buried here make this a popular place for visitors.

Dating from 1803, the cemetery was created on Jesuit land (where Louis XIV's confessor, Father La Chaise once lived). This is also the site of the Communards' last stand in 1871.

Among those buried here are Oscar Wilde, Edith Piaf, the composers Chopin and Poulenc, novelist Marcel Proust, painters Delacroix and Modigliani and architect Baron Haussmann. The tombs of the medieval lovers Abélard and Héloïse, actress Sarah Bernhardt, and the singer Jim Morrison of The Doors, who died in Paris in 1971, lie within its precincts.

Guided tours are available, as is information on the location of the tombs, in case you are planning a leisurely unescorted trip around the cemetery.

Above: There's much to see in this serene cemetery

✉ **Père Lachaise** boulevard de Ménilmontant

☎ 01 55 25 82 10

🌐 **www.pere-lachaise. com**

🕐 Mid–Mar to early Nov, Mon–Fri 8–6, Sat 8:30–6, Sun 9–6; Nov–mid Mar Mon–Fri 8–5:30, Sat 8:30–5:30, Sun 9–5:30

✋ Free

Ⓜ Père Lachaise

Versailles

One of the finest historic buildings in Europe, this magnificent palace shares its name with the wealthy suburb of Paris where it is situated. The Château de Versailles is the ultimate symbol of the grandeur and excesses that prevailed during the reign of King Louis XIV.

Much of the credit for transforming the palace from an old hunting lodge into the vision of splendour that we see today goes to the king, who wanted to move his court to Versailles. Louis XIV turned a humble lodge into a royal residence, seat of the French government and the unofficial capital of France. Although the king came up with the most elaborate of plans, and work commenced in 1661, he never saw it finished. He died in 1715 before the project was complete.

The palace remained a royal residence for more than a century, although it suffered during the Revolution and was left badly damaged and stripped of its furniture and paintings. It was from here that Marie Antoinette fled, but was seized, taken to the Conciergerie and eventually met a bloody end on the guillotine. Versailles will always be remembered for its part in the death of the French monarchy.

For a great many years the palace remained empty, as even Napoleon was unwilling to spend any time here. Ultimately, King Louis-Phillippe declared it a National Museum in 1837.

Above left: Statues and ornamental water gardens near the palace
Above right: The extensive gardens

✉ **Versailles**
Château de Versailles

☎ 01 30 83 78 00

www **www.chateauversailles.fr**

🕐 Apr–Oct, Tue–Sun 9–6:30;
Nov–Mar, Tue–Sun 9–5:30

✋ Chateau moderate, park free

🚈 RER C Versailles Rive Gauche

The palace needs a visit of several hours, if not days, to really appreciate its beauty. See the state apartments (Grands Appartements), which include the partly restored, 70m (230-foot) long Hall of Mirrors (Galérie des Glaces). This is the room in which the Treaty of Versailles that signalled the end of World War I was signed. Its beauty will leave you gasping for more, especially if you see it in the evening, unhindered by the crowds.

The queen's quarters in the northern wing are almost completely covered with gold leaf and have been perfectly restored to resemble their original design. In another section of the palace the Petits Appartements house some of France's most important examples of 18th-century decorative arts. Another eye-opener is the

Hall of Battles, where gigantic paintings celebrate France's military successes.

The 100ha (247-acre) park and gardens at Versailles are as much a part of the experience as the house itself and are the perfect place for a relaxed Sunday morning stroll. The formal gardens are laid out in the classic French style, with geometric pathways, statues, fountains and shrubberies. The English-inspired garden area lies to the north of the Petit Trianon, where Marie Antoinette had a model farm.

Left: A sumptuous bedroom in the chateau
Below: The Grand Trianon was a small palace built by Louis XIV, where he would spend time with his mistress Madame de Montespan

Listings

With thousands of visitors thronging to the city throughout the year, Paris caters for every taste. Hotels range from traditional to modern, and restaurants, cafés and bars abound, offering culinary experiences that are typically French. Paris is a shopper's delight, especially for those who are particular about their brands, and there are countless cultural venues to entertain the young and old – the more energetic can party until the small hours of the morning in a city that's renowned for its nightlife.

Accommodation

Paris offers an exhaustive range of accommodation, for all types of budgets to make a stay in the city memorable. In fact, it is one of the few places in the world where you can stay right in the city centre, close to all the attractions, without having to dig too deeply into your pocket. Staying in the suburbs shouldn't be dismissed, however, as many of these areas abound in leafy avenues, parks and waterways, and are a joy to return to after a busy day in the city.

July and August are when many Parisians head out of the city for holidays by the sea and fewer business people occupy the city centre hotels. These often drop their charges significantly and there are good bargains to be found. In May, June, September and October, however, it's a different story. This is due to the fact that exhibitions and festivals are generally held at this time, and the influx of exhibitors and visitors looking for hotel accommodation grows significantly. Prices and availability of rooms are often at a premium during this time.

Hotels range from privately owned places steeped in character, to larger establishments that are part of a chain. Many of the old traditional ones have been refurbished in recent years to provide mod cons that are now considered a necessity. Many hotels are on the outskirts, but with the métro offering such good service, the journey time into the city centre is just minutes, depending on where you stay. Paris is also filled with 17th- to 19th-century former palaces, and several of these have been converted into luxury hotels. Utterly extravagant and often in the heart of the city, they have hefty price tags, but the experience of staying in such a classically historic French atmosphere might be an irresistible temptation.

Prices

Prices for each hotel are a guide only, and based on a standard double room.

€ under €75
€€ €75–€150
€€€ over €150

AROUND THE TOUR EIFFEL

Grand Hôtel Lévêque €€
A hotel that is hugely popular with English-speaking tourists, so you will need to book at least eight months ahead of your visit. Although the decor is quite ordinary, the hotel is located in the middle of an interesting market.
✉ 29 rue Cler ☎ 01 47 05 49 15
W www.hotel-leveque.com

Hôtel de l'Avre €€
A beautifully presented 26-roomed, two-star hotel set in its own gardens close to the Tour Eiffel.
✉ 21 rue de l'Avre ☎ 01 45 75 31 03
W www.hoteldelavre.com

Hôtel Baltimore €€€
Ideal for families, this hotel is part of the Sofitel chain and is close to the Trocadéro and Tour Eiffel.
✉ 88 bis avenue Kléber ☎ 01 44 34 54 54
W www.sofitel.com

Hôtel du Palais Bourbon €€
Spacious rooms, both single and double, located in an old building next to the Musée Rodin.
✉ 49 rue de Bourgogne ☎ 01 44 11 30 70
W www.hotel-palais-bourbon.com

La Régence Étoile Hôtel €€€
A short walk from the Arc de Triomphe, this hotel has sumptuous lounge areas and modern bedrooms.
✉ 24 avenue Carnot ☎ 01 58 05 42 42
W www.hotelregenceetoile.com

LATIN QUARTER, ST-GERMAIN AND ISLANDS

L'Hôtel €€€
This is truly a place for the well-heeled and the sumptuous decor makes it a wonderful place to stay if you can afford it. From the wallpaper to the furnishings, it is sheer extravagance all the way. The legendary Oscar Wilde died in this iconic hotel. A spectacular spiralling staircase adds to the fantastic interior.
✉ 13 rue des Beaux-Arts ☎ 01 44 41 99 00
W www.l-hotel.com

Hôtel de l'Abbaye Saint-Germain €€€
A former convent, this traditional hotel offers well-presented accommodation in a historic setting close to local attractions.
✉ 10 rue Cassette ☎ 01 45 44 38 11
W www.hotel.abbaye.com

Hôtel d'Angleterre €€
This is a classy and architecturally impressive building and was formerly the premises for the British Embassy. It is luxury personified and an added point of interest is the fact that Ernest Hemingway also stayed here.
✉ 44 rue Jacob ☎ 01 42 60 34 72
W www.hotel-dangleterre.com

Hôtel Claude Bernard €€
With its brightly coloured front façade, this elegant 44-room hotel has a cheerful atmosphere and is a landmark building within the city.
✉ 43 rue des Écoles ☎ 01 43 26 32 52

Hôtel du Collège de France €€
Ideal for exploring the Latin Quarter, this classically-styled 29-room hotel is situated near the Sorbonne.
✉ 7 rue Thénard ☎ 01 43 26 78 36

Hôtel Jardin des Plantes €€
A pretty 33-room hotel with great views over the botanical gardens.
✉ 5 Rue Linné ☎ 01 47 07 06 20
W www.timhotel.com

Hôtel Le Sénat €€€
A very classy hotel, completety refurbished in 2004 and still as good as new. Dark

chocolate leather furnishings with contrasting stripes lend an unusual elegance, placing it among the top-end boutique hotels in the city.

✉ 10 rue de Vaugirard ☎ 01 43 54 54 54
🌐 www.hotelsenat.com

Hôtel Stanislas €

Very good for the budget traveller for whom price is the primary consideration. It is in the heart of Montparnasse and therefore can be noisy, but the rooms are clean and functional.

✉ 5 rue du Montparnasse ☎ 01 45 48 37 05 🌐 www.hotel-stanislas.com

MARAIS AND BASTILLE

Hôtel Caron de Beaumarchais €€

A period hotel, named after the 18th-century French playwright Beaumarchais. It contains some original Louis XVI furniture and other pre-Revolution Paris touches. This is a much sought-after hotel, so book well in advance.

✉ 12 rue Vieille-du-Temple ☎ 01 42 72 34 12 🌐 www.carondebeaumarchais.com

Hôtel Jeanne d'Arc €€

This is another popular hotel, located in a beautiful area, off place du Marché Sainte-Catherine. The rooms on the upper floors have great views.

✉ 3 rue de Jarente ☎ 01 48 87 62 11
🌐 www.hoteljeannedarc.com

Grand Hôtel Malher €€

Well located and welcoming, this hotel with 31 rooms is within an easy walk of the Centre Georges Pompidou.

✉ 5 rue Malher ☎ 01 42 72 60 92
🌐 www.grandhotelmalher.com

Hôtel Pavillon de la Reine €€€

A luxurious hotel with many period features, the Pavillon de la Reine is located in the heart of the Marais district.

✉ 28 place des Vosges ☎ 01 40 29 19 19
🌐 www.pavillon-de-la-reine.fr

Hôtel de la Bretonnerie €€

This is one of the nicest hotels in Paris, right in the heart of the Marais area. All the rooms are designed differently and display great taste, complemented with oak beams and oak furniture. Some feature grand four poster beds and all have beautiful furnishings.

✉ 22 rue Ste Croix de la Bretonnerie
☎ 01 48 87 77 63 🌐 www.bretonnerie.com

Hôtel du Cantal €

If the Musée Picasso is going to be one of your most favourite places to visit in Paris, then this hotel is a good choice on a quiet street behind the museum. In addition, it's elegantly and simply furnished and has a café-bar where you can get breakfast and dinner.

✉ 7 rue des Vertus ☎ 01 42 77 65 52

Hôtel de la Place des Vosges €€

This charming 17th-century townhouse hotel is in a quiet street conveniently located close to the museums of the Marais district.

✉ 12 rue de Birague ☎ 01 42 72 60 46
🌐 www.hotelplacedesvosges.com

LOUVRE AND CHAMPS-ÉLYSÉES

Hôtel Franklin Roosevelt €€€

With its dark wood furnishings, red fabrics and atmospheric lighting, this hotel oozes sophistication and luxury.

✉ 18 rue Clément Marot ☎ 01 53 57 49 50
🌐 www.hroosevelt.com

Hôtel de Lille €

For a very reasonable price at this hotel, you will get rooms that are pleasantly decorated, some of them with their own toilet. Breakfast is not served here so you will have to find a café to start your day.

Bear in mind that there are five floors – and no lift.

✉ 8 rue du Pélican ☎ 01 42 33 33 42

Hôtel Molière €€€

A beautifully presented hotel that is conveniently sited within easy walking distance of the Opéra Palais Garnier and the Musée du Louvre.

✉ 21 rue Molière ☎ 01 42 96 22 01
🆆 www.hotel-moliere.fr

Hôtel Queen Mary €€€

A small, classically French-styled hotel that is well located for exploring the city centre. It has 35 rooms and 1 suite.

✉ 9 rue Sainte-Beuve ☎ 01 45 48 20 07

MONTMARTRE

Hôtel André Gill €€

A pleasing, small 33-roomed hotel set around a courtyard brimming over with character.

✉ 4 rue André Gill ☎ 01 42 62 48 48

Hôtel Bonséjour €

This is a great location and the rooms come at a great price for budget travellers. Located on a slope, it may require a little effort to reach the hotel but once you are there, the owners are eager to to give you a comfortable stay.

✉ 11 rue Burq ☎ 01 42 54 22 53
🆆 www.hotel-bonsejour-montmartre.fr

L'Ermitage €€

A family-run hotel with an old-world ambience created by its heritage decor. Some of the flowery wallpaper is truly beautiful and the hotel's location on a hill affords fine views over the city.

✉ 24 rue Lamarck ☎ 01 42 64 79 22
🆆 www.ermitagesacrecoeur.fr

Hôtel Lorette Opéra €€€

One of the Best Western group of hotels, this one is peaceful, intimate and friendly.

The rooms are nicely designed and comfortable and the location is unbeatable, between Opéra and Montmartre. There is also a charming breakfast room.

✉ 36 rue Notre Dame de Lorette
☎ 01 42 85 18 81
🆆 www.bestwestern.com

Hôtel Marclau €

Though cheaply priced, this hotel is located in a nice, quiet part of Montmartre. All the rooms are clean and spacious, and if you pay extra you can have your own shower and/or toilet.

✉ 78 rue du Faubourg Poissonnière ☎ 01 47 70 73 50 🆆 www.hotel-marclau.com

Hôtel Terminus Nord €€€

Part of the Libertel group, this is a luxury hotel with touches of Victoriana. It is conveniently located directly opposite the Gare du Nord, and is a comfortable place to stay.

✉ 12 blvd de Denain ☎ 01 42 80 20 00

Timhotel Montmartre €

Located close to the Sacré-Coeur, this popular and well-presented hotel is in the heart of Montmartre. You can walk out and watch pavement artists at work and even sit for a portrait yourself.

✉ 11 rue Ravignan ☎ 01 42 55 74 79
🆆 www.timhotel.com

Restaurants

Parisians have long had a reputation for being gourmands. Every resident has his/her favourite bakery from which they buy their baguettes and croissants. One traditional bread, *Poilâne*, named after the family of bakers, is the favourite of film stars around the world, and is booked on order as soon it is baked every weekend. Other gourmet foods associated with Paris include *fois gras*, truffles and *fromages* (cheeses). Every corner of the city has its selection of speciality outlets from which you can pick up your choice of these individual items if you're on the move. To complement the food, there is an unbeatable variety of delectable wines and champagnes. But apart from such self-service choices, Paris has thousands of restaurants catering for every taste, where you can enjoy a leisurely meal. Whether the choice is for Oriental cuisine, Indian, Malaysian, Thai, Italian, Mexican or English, *à la carte* and classic French, the city has hundreds of eateries in each category. Crêperies and cafés, too, offer a splendid choice of lighter dishes.

Most restaurants in the areas immediately adjacent to the top tourist attractions, shopping areas and central avenues tend to be packed with tourists rather than locals. Those located off the beaten track and in residential areas are frequented predominantly by residents of the city. Choosing the latter can be a delightful way to enjoy the atmosphere of authentic Parisian living.

Restaurants generally have price bands. It is cheaper, for instance, to sit inside than out in the open, especially along avenues such as the Champs-Élysées. Similarly, choosing the *plat du jour* (dish of the day), which usually consists of a starter, main course and a light dessert, can be the best value. Choosing from the menu offers a far wider choice, and restaurants invariably offer a good wine list.

Prices

Prices for each restaurant are a guide only, and based on a 3-course meal from the menu for one person.

€ under €20
€€ €20–€80
€€€ over €80

AROUND THE TOUR EIFFEL

L'Affrioloé €€

A popular bistro-style restaurant with a modernist feel, l'Affrioloé is close to the Tour Eiffel and serves unusual French dishes and a great choice of wines. This is a good choice for a nice lunch with friends.
✉ 17 rue Malar ☎ 01 44 18 31 33
🕐 Lunch and evening dining, except weekends

Altitude 95 €€

Along with the famous Jules Verne, Altitude 95 is a restaurant within the Tour Eiffel. Despite its fabulous location and views, it is surprisingly inexpensive to dine here.
✉ 1st level Tour Eiffel ☎ 01 45 55 20 04
🕐 Daily for lunch and evening dining

L'Ami Jean €€

With a good choice of dishes from the Basque region on the menu, including veal, beef and seafood, and an especially good wine list, L'Ami Jean is a good place to enjoy a fine meal.
✉ 27 rue Malar ☎ 01 47 05 86 89
🕐 Lunch and evening dining, except Sun and Mon

Benkay €€

For lovers of Japanese food, Benkay offers an extensive menu of authentic dishes, from sushi to teppanyaki. It is located within the Novotel Paris Tour Eiffel and has panoramic views of the area.
✉ 61 quai de Grenelle ☎ 01 40 58 21 26
🕐 Daily for lunch and evening dining

Le Ciel de Paris €€

This elegant restaurant on the 56th floor of the Tour Montparnasse has the distinction of being Europe's highest eatery. The views are among the best in Paris.
✉ 33 avenue du Maine ☎ 01 40 64 77 64
🆆 www.cieldeparis.com 🕐 Daily for lunch and evening dining

La Ferme St-Simon €€

A menu of classic à la carte French cuisine and an impressive wine list make this traditional country-style restaurant, complete with exposed beams, popular with visitors and residents alike.
✉ 6 rue de St-Simon ☎ 01 45 48 35 74
🕐 Daily for lunch and evening dining, except Sun

Il Gallo Nero €€

An atmospheric Italian restaurant, Il Gallo Nero has a modern decor and a competitively priced menu full of classic dishes from Italy, with a good wine list.
✉ 35 rue Raymond Losserand
☎ 01 42 18 00 38 🆆 www.il-gallo-nero.com
🕐 Daily for lunch and evening dining, except Sun

Goa €

With a menu of curries, tikkas and numerous other dishes to tempt the tastebuds, this traditional Indian restaurant is close to the Tour Eiffel and is always packed with diners.
✉ 19 rue Augereau ☎ 01 45 55 26 20
🕐 Daily for lunch and evening dining, except Sun

Thoumieux €€

Characterised by its lavish decor of rich fabrics and mirrors, this classic 85-year-old French restaurant serves hearty dishes that have stood the test of time in kitchens throughout the country.
✉ 79 rue St-Dominique ☎ 01 47 05 49 75
🆆 www.thoumieux.com 🕐 Daily for lunch and evening dining

LATIN QUARTER, ST-GERMAIN AND ISLANDS

Alcazar €€
This lively restaurant, with a great fish menu and lounge bar, is famed for being designer Terence Conran's Parisian business. You will be among the chic diners of the city.
✉ 62 rue Mazarine ☎ 01 53 10 19 99
🕐 Daily for lunch and evening dining through to 2am

Allard €€
Close to Notre-Dame and the Conciergerie, the Allard captures the authentic feel of bistro-style dining. The menu features classic French cuisine.
✉ 41 rue At-André des Arts ☎ 01 43 26 48 23 🕐 Daily for lunch and evening dining, except Sun

Brasserie Balzar €€
If you fancy hearty French food, such as *cassoulet*, a tasty casserole of sausages and beans that has been a staple of kitchens throughout the country for generations, then head for Brasserie Balzar.
✉ 49 rue des Écoles ☎ 01 43 54 13 67
🕐 Daily for lunch and evening dining

Brasserie Lipp €€
This 19th-century eatery oozes period charm which, together with its classic French menu and wines, makes it a popular venue for the city's celebrities.
✉ 151 boulevard Saint-Germain ☎ 01 45 48 53 91 🖳 www.brasserie-lipp.fr
🕐 Daily for lunch and evening dining

La Coupole €€
A fashionable 1920s brasserie that is frequented by residents, business people and tourists, it serves a menu of classics such as veal with tarragon and *fois gras*.
✉ 102 boulevard du Montparnasse
☎ 01 43 20 14 20 🕐 Daily for lunch and evening dining

La Ferrandaise €€
A fashionable country-style restaurant close to the Jardin du Luxembourg, La Ferrandaise offers a menu of French classics at good prices, complemented by some truly fine wines.
✉ 8 rue de Vaugirard ☎ 01 43 26 36 36
🖳 www.laferrandaise.com 🕐 Daily for lunch and evening dining, except Sun and Mon, Sat evening only

Jacques Cagna €€€
You must book ahead to dine at this hugely fashionable and upmarket eatery. An ever-changing menu of French classic dishes and an elegant decor ensure it remains a popular place to dine.
✉ 14 rue des Grands-Augustins ☎ 01 43 26 49 39 🖳 www.jacquescagna.com
🕐 Daily for lunch and evening dining, except Mon and Sat lunch and all day Sun

Le Petit Saint Benoît €
With its period decor, hearty menu, and friendly staff, the Le Petit Saint Benoît is a great place to enjoy an inexpensive meal in an atmospheric setting.
✉ 4 rue Saint Benoît ☎ 01 42 60 27 92
🖳 www.petit-st-benoit.com 🕐 Daily for lunch and evening dining, except Sun

La Tour d'Argent €€€
With a great view across the 18th-century houses of the Parisian elite, this popular restaurant on the Île Saint-Louis serves fine à la carte cuisine.
✉ 15–17 quai de la Tournelle ☎ 01 43 54 23 31 🖳 www.latourdargent.com
🕐 Daily for lunch and evening dining, except all day Mon, and Tue lunch

Yugaraj €€
A lengthy menu with some of the best curries in town, the Yugaraj is an elegant Indian restaurant within easy reach of the Musée du Louvre and the Conciergerie.
✉ 14 rue Dauphine ☎ 01 43 26 44 91

www.yugaraj.com ⏰ Daily for lunch and evening dining, except Mon and Tue lunch

MARAIS AND BASTILLE

404 €€
Lovers of Moroccan and other north African cuisine will be hard pushed to find a better restaurant with such a comprehensive menu. The decor of this atmospheric eatery is pure Berber.
✉ 69 rue des Gravilliers ☎ 01 42 74 57 81
⏰ Daily for lunch and evening dining

Au Pied de Cochon €€
Set right near the Jardin du Forum des Halles, this classically-modern brasserie is popular with tourists and residents. The menu is lively and tasty.
✉ 6 rue Coquillère ☎ 01 40 13 77 00
www.pieddecochon.com

La Baracane €€
With a menu focusing on traditional cuisine from the Gascony region, including delicious duck recipes handed down through the generations, La Baracane is a popular bistro in the heart of the Bastille district.
✉ 38 rue des Tournelles ☎ 01 42 71 43 33

Bel Canto €€
Famous for the way it creates an atmosphere through Italian operatic arias, this elegant restaurant has a full menu of classic dishes and wines from Italy.
✉ 72 quai de l'Hôtel de Ville ☎ 01 42 78 30 18 ⏰ Daily for evening dining only

Benoît €€€
An Alain Ducasse restaurant where the menu features top-notch classic French cuisine and fine wines. This luxurious restaurant is always full and advance booking is advised.
✉ 20 rue Saint-Martin ☎ 01 42 72 25 76
⏰ Daily for lunch and evening dining

Bofinger €€
Believed to be the oldest restaurant in Paris, with a history going back to 1864, this lavish eatery is characterised by chandeliers and a glass dome. A combination of classic and contemporary French.
✉ 5 rue de la Bastille ☎ 01 42 72 87 82
www.bofingerparis.com ⏰ Daily for lunch and evening dining

Clown Bar €€
A fun and lively eatery with a clown-inspired antique decor, the Clown Bar serves a menu of French dishes and fine wines.
✉ 114 rue Amalot ☎ 01 43 55 87 35
⏰ Daily for lunch and evening dining

Les Grandes Marches €€
Known for its unusual twist to classic French dishes and its good selection of seafood, Les Grandes Marches is a popular eatery in the Bastille district.
✉ 6 place de la Bastille ☎ 01 43 42 90 32
⏰ Daily for lunch and evening dining

Ma Bourgogne €€
An informal yet elegant eatery that serves hearty dishes with a contemporary French twist, Ma Bourgogne is an ideal place for a meal with friends.
✉ 19 place des Vosges ☎ 01 42 78 44 64
⏰ Daily for lunch and evening dining

La Tête Ailleurs €€
A Mediterranean-themed decor, complete with stone walls and plants, and a menu of classic dishes from the region, make this eatery near the river a must.
✉ 20 rue Beautreillis ☎ 01 42 72 47 80
⏰ Daily for lunch and evening dining, except Sat lunch and all day Sun

LOUVRE AND CHAMPS-ÉLYSÉES

6 New York €€
A swish, brightly-coloured modern decor characterises this eatery, close to the

Parc Monceau, that serves internationally inspired cuisine, popular with globetrotters.
✉ **6 avenue de New York** ☎ **01 40 70 03 30**
🕐 Daily for lunch and evening dining, except Sat lunch and all day Sun

Café Marly €€
A café-restaurant with a luxurious feel and a good menu, the Café Marly is housed in the Musée du Louvre and has a terrace that overlooks the glass pyramid.
✉ **93 rue de Rivoli** ☎ **01 49 26 06 60**
🕐 Daily from 8am through to the early hours.

Carre des Feuil-Lants €€
Famous chef Alain Dutournier is the force behind this popular restaurant close to the Jardin des Tuileries. His menu has classic dishes from the Gascony region.
✉ **14 rue de Castiglione** ☎ **01 42 86 82 82**
🕐 Daily for lunch and evening dining, except Sat and Sun

Le Céladon €€€
A centrally located restaurant close to the Opéra Palais Garnier, Le Céladon serves up classic French cuisine in an elegant interior.
✉ **15 rue Daunou** ☎ **01 47 03 40 42**
🌐 www.leceladon.com 🕐 Daily for lunch and evening dining, except Sat and Sun

Guy Savoy €€€
Booking is a must if you wish to feast on renowned chef Guy Savoy's truly inspired French cuisine. This restaurant is among the finest gourmet eateries in Paris.
✉ **18 rue Troyon** ☎ **01 43 80 40 61**
🌐 www.guysavoy.com 🕐 Daily for lunch and evening dining, except for Sat lunch and all day Sun and Mon

Man Ray (World Place) €€
This restaurant is famous for its French menu with a Japanese and Thai influence, its lavish Asian themed decor, and the fact that it was opened by actors Johnny Depp, Sean Penn and John Malkovich. You may

even see a famous face here.
✉ **34 rue Marbeuf** ☎ **01 56 88 36 36**
🕐 Daily for lunch and evening dining

Le Senderens €€€
Top Michelin chef Alain Senderens opened this elegant restaurant a short distance from the Champs-Élysées a while back. It serves the finest French gourmet cuisine.
✉ **9 place de la Madeleine** ☎ **01 42 65 22 90** 🕐 Daily for lunch and evening dining

Spoon €€€
An unusual menu with dishes from around the world characterises this upmarket bistro, opened by top chef Alain Ducasse.
✉ **14 rue de Marignan** ☎ **01 40 76 34 44**
🕐 Daily for lunch and evening dining, except Sat lunch and Sun

Taillevent €€€
For especially elegant surroundings in which to enjoy a special meal, or some of the finest French cuisine to be found in Paris, head for Taillevent, located near the Arc de Triomphe.
✉ **15 rue Lamennais** ☎ **01 44 95 15 01**
🌐 www.taillevent.com 🕐 Daily for lunch and evening dining, except Sat and Sun

MONTMARTRE

Café Burq €€
Popular with the young and trendy set, this contemporary bistro-style bar-cum-restaurant serves a good choice of international cuisine.
✉ **6 rue Burq** ☎ **01 42 52 81 27**
🕐 Daily for evening dining, except Sun

Chez Grisette €€
Set in a building full of character, not far from the Sacré-Coeur, Chez Grisette offers a classic seasonal French menu.
✉ **14 rue Houdon** ☎ **01 42 62 04 80**
🌐 www.chez-grisette.fr 🕐 Daily for evening dining, except Sat and Sun

Le Ch'Ti Catalan €€

The Le Ch'Ti Catalan serves an unusual combination of French and Catalonian cuisine, which is lovingly created by its dedicated owners.

✉ 4 rue Navarin ☎ 01 44 63 04 33
🕐 Daily for lunch and evening dining, except Sat lunch and all day Sun

L'Épicerie €€

With a decor and menu inspired by the Tuscan region in Italy, L'Épicerie is a great place to enjoy authentic pasta dishes complemented by the finest of Italian wines.

✉ 51 rue des Martyrs ☎ 01 48 78 07 50
🕐 Daily for lunch and evening dining

Le Progrès €

A lively little café in the heart of the Montmartre district, Le Progrès has an unpretentious menu of snacks, light lunches and *plats du jour*. It is justly popular with both locals and visitors.

✉ 7 rue des Trois-Frères ☎ 01 42 64 07 37
🕐 Daily for lunch and evening meals until late

Rose Bakery €€

Famous for its good selection of cakes, pastries and desserts made from organic ingredients, this English-inspired bakery and tea shop is an ideal stop for a refreshment break, especially if you have a sweet tooth.

✉ 46 rue des Martyrs ☎ 01 42 82 12 80
🕐 Daily for snacks, lunch and early evening dining

Velly €€

The sign of a good restaurant is when it is well frequented by locals, and Velly certainly falls into that category. Contemporary French and international dishes are served here at reasonable prices.

✉ 52 rue Lamartine ☎ 01 48 78 60 05
🕐 Daily for lunch and evening dining, except Sat and Sun

FURTHER AFIELD

Byblos €

For good Greek and French cuisine, try Byblos when you're in the western part of Paris. It comes at a reasonable price.

✉ 14 rue Saint-Severin ☎ 01 44 07 11 11
🕐 Daily for lunch and evening dining

La Gare €

No transport problems here, as it is at the station. Super lunches are served on a lovely terrace when the weather permits and there's also a bar.

✉ 19 chaussée de la Muette ☎ 01 48 78 60 05 🕐 Daily for lunch and evening dining; bar open from noon to 2am

Shopping

Paris is a shopper's delight. Everything from fashion and food to antiques and cosmetics can be found in the avenues and marketplaces that abound in the city. In this fashion capital of Europe, if you're looking for haute couture the 1st and 8th *arrondissements* are your best bet. Saint-Germain-des-Prés is great fun to explore if you have the time, and do not necessarily wish to buy. Here you will find narrow streets with irresistible souvenirs to take home or just admire in the shop window.

You must also visit a couple of markets, which have an atmosphere all of their own. Perhaps most memorable are the food markets, which will flood your senses with wonderful sights, smells and colours. Best buys include genuine *haute couture* fashion for men and women (although clothing is available in all price brackets) along with lingerie for which the French are famous, perfumes and cosmetics, famous French wines, food, and stationery. French stationery, often using handmade paper, makes an ideal memento of the city. Parisians are known for their love of music too, and many shops offer an exhaustive selection of CDs by French and fashionable world artists.

AROUND THE TOUR EIFFEL

Annick Goutal
You really shouldn't leave Paris without buying a bottle of perfume, and if you feel like pampering yourself, then do try one of the Goutal brand of lime and lemony ones, all made from natural essences. An all-time favourite is Eau d'Hadrien, and for men it's Eau de Monsieur.
✉ 12 place Saint-Sulpice ⏰ Mon–Sat 10–7

Editions de Parfums Frédéric Malle

A unique source of perfumes, where professional parfumeurs create their own brands under the name of this establishment. And if you really want a perfume that no one else in the world will have, you can even create your own mix, but remember, it comes at a hefty price!

✉ 37 rue de Grenelle 🖳 www.editionsdeparfums.com 🕔 Mon–Sat 11–7; closed two weeks in Aug

Galerie Maeght

Graphic and other designers love the Galerie Maeght, as does anyone looking for quality printed items – posters, postcards, stationery, and sheets of handmade paper. All are stocked in colourful abundance.

✉ 42 rue du Bac 🕔 Mon 10–6, Tue–Sat 9:30–7

Le Bon Marché Rive Gauche

A large modernist-inspired store located not far from the Tour Eiffel, this has some beautifully presented upmarket goods on display. There's an in-store beauty shop called the Théâtre de la Beauté, along with a food hall, La Grande Épicerie, which stocks delicacies from around the world.

✉ 22 rue de Sèvres 🖀 01 44 39 80 00 🖳 www.lebonmarche.fr 🕔 Daily 9:30–7, Thur 10–9, Sat 9:30–8; closed Sun

The Conran Shop

Located in a building designed by Gustave Eiffel, famed of course for the Tour Eiffel, designer Sir Terence Conran's exquisite shop attracts Parisians in droves. Displays of accessories for the home are eye-catching with their flamboyant modernist designs and refined materials.

✉ 117 rue du Bac 🖀 01 42 84 10 01 🕔 Daily 10–7, Sat 10–7:30; closed Sun

Galerie Captier

Stepping into the Galerie Captier is rather like entering another world. Owners Bernard and Sylvie Captier stock an amazing range of 17th- to 19th-century Chinese and Japanese furniture and screens, along with unusual works of art, that they have personally sourced from the Orient.

✉ 33 rue de Beaune 🖀 01 42 61 00 57 🕔 Daily 11–7; closed Mon and Sun

LATIN QUARTER, ST-GERMAIN AND ISLANDS

Album

Look for old editions here, and if you are into comic books, then there are five different comic shops in this block of Dante houses.

✉ 6–8 rue Dante, 60 rue Monsieur le Prince 🖳 www.album.fr 🕔 Tue–Sat 10–8

Boulinier

Here you have a good chance of finding that old – or not so old – CD or book that you have been looking for. This is perhaps the best secondhand book and CD shop in this part of Paris – much too tempting, so be prepared to spend!

✉ 20 boulevard St-Michel 🕔 Mon–Thu 10–11, Fri and Sat 10–midnight, Sun 2–midnight

Colette

This is not just a shop, but one of the famous "sights" of Paris. Colette gives you the best of haute couture design, accessories and other decorative items, all superbly displayed, and, unexpectedly, an unlikely selection of exotic mineral waters from all over the world. You could easily spend the best part of a day here browsing the selection.

✉ 213 rue Saint-Honoré 🖳 www.colette.fr 🕔 Mon–Sat 10:30–7:30

Dalloyau

Famed for its tempting displays and vast selection of fine pastries and cakes, Dalloyau is a magnet for anyone in the throes of planning a party or a picnic. Call in on the way to the Jardin du Luxembourg, which is opposite.

✉ 2 place Edmond Rostand ☎ 01 43 29 31 10 🕐 Daily 9–8:30

Galerie Documents

Art lovers and collectors of old prints, postcards, posters and the like find this temporary home of archival material an absolute mecca. Items range mainly from 1890 to 1940 and include the works of such masters as Toulouse-Lautrec and Alphonse Mucha.

✉ 53 rue de Seine ☎ 01 43 54 50 68 🕐 Open Tue–Sat 10.30–7, Mon 2:30–7

Ikuo

Hundreds of colourful, innovatively designed trinkets, such as earrings and pendants, are displayed here. It's a good place to look for co-ordinating finishing touches.

✉ 11 rue des Grands-Augustins ☎ 01 43 29 56 39 🕐 Daily 9:30am–11:45pm, except Sun until 7:45pm

La Chambre Claire

This shop sells a wide variety of books on photography, many of them in English. You will also find a small collection of interesting photographs.

✉ 14 rue St-Sulpice 🕐 Tue–Sat 10–7

La Hune

A popular haunt of the literary and arty fraternity of the Saint-Germain-des-Prés area, who can often be found happily browsing here late into the night or on a Sunday, La Hune is a large bookshop that specialises in architecture and art.

✉ 170 boulevard Saint-Germain ☎ 01 45 48 35 85 🕐 Daily 9:30–11:45, Sun until 7:45pm

Librarie Bonaparte

A fabulous collection of books and some prints on the performing arts – dance, music, drama, and even puppets.

✉ 19 boulevard Raspail ☎ 01 47 03 40 12

🌐 www.bonaparte-spectacles.com 🕐 Sep–Jun Tue–Sat 10–7; Jul and Aug 10–1, 2–7

Marché aux Fleurs

Husbands, boyfriends, housewives, plant lovers and landscape designers, often from outside the country, flock here for the vast choice of flowers, plants and herbs and ideas for garden or event design.

✉ place Louis Lépine 🕐 Mon–Sun 8–7:30

Marie Mercié

An elegant little shop, not far from the riverside, that oozes French chic, Marie Mercié has an eye-catching display of women's hats for every occasion. There are large ones with feathers for a day at the races, theatrical versions and everyday classics.

✉ 23 rue Saint-Sulpice ☎ 01 43 26 45 83 🕐 Daily 9:30–7; closed Sun

Rue Mouffetard

For an intoxicating whiff of fresh basil or tarragon, for emerald green avocadoes and blood red tomatoes, or for an amazing choice of cheeses and cold cuts, you simply must stroll down this quaint and picturesque street, where you can also take a café break.

✉ rue Mouffetard 🕐 Daily early morning to late night

Shakespeare and Company

When you are tired of sightseeing, this is a delightful little place for a browse. There is a small library, and in the shop below you might be lucky enough to discover that rare out-of-print book.

✉ 37 rue de la Bûcherie ☎ 01 43 25 40 93 🕐 Daily noon–midnight

Sonia Rykiel

A fashion name to reckon with, this is a popular place to add that special something to your wardrobe.

✉ 175 boulevard Saint-Germain ☎ 01 49 54 60 60

MARAIS AND BASTILLE

Antik Batik
Exotic designs from the East – batik, handmade embroideries, sequins, brocades and glitter, as well as seductive lingerie.
✉ 18 rue de Turenne 📞 01 44 78 02 00
🕐 Daily 9:30–7; closed Sun

BHV
All kinds of goods are available here – ready-to-wear clothes, pots and pans, stationery, canned foods – all sold at reasonable rates.
✉ 52 rue de Rivoli 📞 01 42 74 90 00
🕐 Mon–Sat, 9.30–7.30, until 9 on Wed

Dehillerin
Check out the latest in design for your new kitchen or in order to upgrade the old one. The catalogue is worth keeping for the mail order service.
✉ 18 rue Coquillière 📞 01 42 36 53 13
🕐 Mon–Sat, 9:30–7:30, until 9 on Wed

Forum des Halles
Step into the underground chambers of the Forum Des Halles and you will be greeted by a vast array of some 50 or more designer shops. From classics to ultra modern, there are garments on four floors to suit everyone's taste.
✉ 1–7 rue Pierre-Lescot 🕐 Daily 9:30–7; closed Sun

La Droguerie
Set in the heart of the fashionable Marais district, La Droguerie has an amazing selection of beads, wools, fabrics, ribbons and threads to create soft furnishings and accessories for the home, make fashion jewellery or to remodel fashion items.
✉ 9 rue du Jour 📞 01 45 08 93 27 🕐 Daily 9:30–7; closed Sun

Oliviers & Co
For anyone who adores cooking or dipping with olive oil, Oliviers & Co will amaze with its range of products from around the world. There are fine extra virgin oils from the Mediterranean and further afield, as well as olive oil-based appetisers and accessories too.
✉ 47 rue Vielle-du-Temple 📞 01 42 74 38 40 🕐 Daily 11–8

LOUVRE AND CHAMPS-ÉLYSÉES

À la Mère de Famille
Entering the À la Mère de Famille is a little like stepping back in time. An original 18th-century grocery shop, complete with shop window and shelves, it offers a tempting selection of deli goods, sweets and chocolate.
✉ 35 rue du Faubourg 📞 01 47 70 83 69
🕐 Daily 9:30–7, except Sun

Chanel
You have to enter the hallowed portals of this iconic shop, if only to tell the folks back home that you were here, literally walking the footsepts of Coco Chanel. It's a genuine touch of class.
✉ 29 rue Cambon 📞 01 42 86 28 00

Chalcographie du Louvre
This interesting shop within the Musée du Louvre complex offers engravings that have been hand printed from the museum's collection of artists' plates. There are around 13,000 to choose from.
✉ Musée du Louvre 📞 01 40 20 59 35
🕐 Daily 9:30–7, except Sun, until 9:30pm Mon and Wed

Institut Géographique National
As you might expect, this is the place for maps and any other serious material on travel, such as guidebooks. It is the official source for maps of France and you won't find a better selection than in the institute.
✉ 107 rue la Boétie 🌐 www.ign.fr
🕐 Mon–Fri 9:30–7, Sat 11–12:30, 2–6:30

Librairie le Moniteur

A mecca for architects, with an unbelievable range of books in English on the subject, historic and contemporary. They even have their own magazine on public building projects which detail all the wonderful buildings that have changed the face of Paris in more recent decades.

✉ 7 place de l'Odéon 🕙 Mon–Sat 10–7

Le Louvre des Antiquaires

An exploration of the 250 shops here can be confusing but exciting – there is a bewildering range of furniture, jewellery and other *objets d'art*.

✉ 2 place du Palais-Royal, opposite the Louvre ☎ 01 42 97 27 00 🕙 Daily 9:30–7, except Sun, until 9:30pm Mon and Wed

Louis Vuitton

It's one of the 'sights' of Paris, so do visit it – if you can get in! In fact, more than a shop, Louis Vuitton is a whole new concept in retail design. On the Champs Élysées, this mega-store is like a part of the grand avenue itself, and after battling the crowds, you'll be treated to a regular feast of designer bags and belts.

✉ 101 avenue des Champs Élysées ☎ 01 53 57 52 00 🕙 Daily 10:30–7:30

Si Tu Veux

A wonderful shop for children, or for adults remembering their childhood with nostalgia, Si Tu Veux is a toy shop with both contemporary and classic playthings and games. There is even a section devoted entirely to teddy bears.

✉ 68 Galerie Vivienne ☎ 01 42 60 59 97 🕙 Daily 9:30–7; closed Sun

MONTMARTRE

American Retro

You could be forgiven for thinking this shop would contain all things American, but in fact the retro refers to its vintage style clothing, such as flapper dresses, and its classic shoes.

✉ 8 rue des Abbessess ☎ 01 42 54 01 10 🕙 Daily 9:30–7; closed Sun

Biberon & Fils

If you are looking for bags you will be more than pleasantly surprised when you walk in Biberon & Fils, and it's very likely you will walk out with a good buy. The quality of the leather is impressive and there is a large selection of classy styles to tempt you.

✉ 334 rue Saint-Honoré 🕙 Mon–Sat 10:30–6:30

Boulangerie Delmontel

Chef Arnaud Delmontel, who is the force behind this beautiful little bakery and patisserie in the heart of Montmartre, is an award-winner, and famous for his Chocomiss, a sumptuous chocolate ganache and raspberry mousse cake flavoured with almond.

✉ 39 rue des Martyrs ☎ 01 48 78 29 33 🕙 Daily 9:30–7; closed Sun

Jamin-Puech

If you're searching for the perfect match for a special evening dress, look no further than Jamin-Puech, where you'll find gorgeous bags, scarves and textiles, all of which give this shop an exclusive character.

✉ 61 rue d'Hauteville ☎ 01 40 22 08 32 ⌨ www.jamin-puech.com 🕙 Tue–Sat 10:30–7

Librairie des Abbesses

This is a delight for bookworms. It's a little bookshop that seemingly sells every book ever written in French. The Librairie des Abbesses is a popular haunt of both literary types and students from the Montmartre district.

✉ 30 rue Yvonne le Tac ☎ 01 46 06 84 30 🕙 Daily 9:30–7; closed Sun

Spree

A very stylish shop, specialising in designer clothes but also stocking other design items such as pieces of furniture or decorative accessories. The decor is stunning, with regularly changing shop window displays. The clothing is, unsurprisingly, in the higher price category.

✉ **16 rue de la Vieuville**
☎ **01 42 23 41 40** 🖥 **www.spree.fr**
🕐 **Mon 2–7, Tue 11–7:30**

Tati

If you run out of clothes for some reason or wish to pick up something really reasonable, Tati is a good place to look. It offers huge variety and prices are exceptionally reasonable. It also stocks other useful items. You will recognise the shop by its gingham theme. There are several branches across the city.

✉ **5 rue Belhomme** 🖥 **www.tati.fr**
🕐 **Mon–Fri 10–7, Sat 9:15–7**

Virginie Monroe

This shop stocks trinkets and unusual jewellery made of glass, semi-precious stones, feathers and sequins, all with a lot of glitter for those who like to jazz up. It's moderately priced.

✉ **30 rue de Charonne**
🕐 **Mon–Sat 11:30–8**

FURTHER AFIELD

Galerie Patrick Séguin

A fine collection of furniture and objects from the 1950s, including pieces by Le Corbusier and Jean Prouvé – though not everthing is for sale. If you like this, there's another showroom nearby in rue des Taillandiers.

✉ **34 rue des Taillandiers**
☎ **01 47 00 32 35**
🖥 **www.patrickseguin.com**
🕐 **Tue–Sat noon–7**

Le Viaduc des Arts

This is a beautifully restored crafts centre where, in a warren of shops under the arches of the old railway viaduct, you can see the craftsmen at work. From textiles to metalwork, ceramics and sculpture – it's all here.

✉ **9–129 avenue Daumesnil** 🕐 **Mon–Sat 10:30–7:30**

Entertainment

Paris is a city that doesn't sleep. There are clubs, especially the more exotic ones in the Montmartre district, that stay open all night, and even museums that are open round-the-clock during the special festival, La Nuit des Musées, which is held in May every year. You can combine an evening cruise on the Seine with a meal and entertainment of your choice, or you might prefer to sit back and relax with friends after a day's sightseeing in one of the chic lounge bars that stay open until the small hours.

A trip to the theatre or to see an opera at venues such as the Opéra Palais Garnier or the Opéra Bastille is also popular, while art galleries and museums host special events and festivals often well into the evening. Such an experience can be even more memorable with a meal before or after the visit. Paris has several excellent film theatres too, where the newest releases can be seen alongside cult classics. The city's cafés transform from simple eateries during the day to lively, atmospheric venues for jazz and contemporary musicians during the evening. There are also plenty of clubs for high energy dancing to all kinds of music, from R&B to house.

For quieter evening experiences, many of the parks are open until late, offering the chance for a pleasant stroll, and sports centres for late-night games of tennis or squash.

Two publications list details of a wide selection of Paris' entertainment options: *Pariscope* and *L'Officiel des Spectacles*, both out on Wednesday. There is also the weekly magazine *Zurban*, which is very informative.

AROUND THE TOUR EIFFEL

La Pagode
Famed for showing an extensive range of films, from contemporary productions to cult classics, La Pagode is a film theatre housed in an oriental-style pagoda not far from the Tour Eiffel.

✉ 57 bis rue de Babylone ☎ 01 45 55 48 48 🕐 Variable, according to the schedule

Palais de Tokyo

Housed within a modernist concrete building, as befits its arty theme, this gallery hosts an ever-changing array of contemporary art exhibitions, festivals, films and concerts.

✉ 13 avenue du Président Wilson
☎ 01 47 23 54 01 ⊕ Daily noon–midnight, except Mon

Le Petit Journal Montparnasse

This is a very popular nightspot, where the emphasis is on good food and top-notch jazz from France's leading musicians. The Petit Journal Montparnasse is not far from the Tour Montparnasse, and is a sister venue to Le Petit Journal Saint Michel.

✉ 13 rue Commandant-Mouchette ☎ 01 43 21 56 70 ⊕ Daily, except Sun; times vary

LATIN QUARTER, ST-GERMAIN AND ISLANDS

L'Arlequin

A magnet for film buffs. Classic films show every Sunday at 11am, followed by a discussion in the café opposite.

✉ 36 rue de Rennes ☎ 01 01 45 44 28 80
⊕ Sun 11am; check for other times

La Balle au Bond

Offering one of the best ways to see Paris by night, La Balle au Bond is a floating restaurant, concert and theatre venue on the Seine that hosts regular musical evenings and productions. It is especially famed for its great jazz events.

✉ quai Malaquais, near Pont des Arts (Apr–Oct); quai de la Tournelle, near Notre Dame cathedral (Nov–Mar) ☎ 01 40 46 85 12 ⊕ Daily; times vary

MK2 Bibliothèque

You are spoilt for choice with 14 screens in this creatively designed venue. There is also a café to relax in before or after viewing a classic French film, or a foreign-language

(dubbed) movie. You should find something to interest you here.

✉ 128–162 avenue de France ☎ 08 92 69 84 84 ⊕ Daily; check for times

Musée National du Moyen Age-Thermes de Cluny

Lovers of classical and chamber music will find an extensive programme of events at this beautiful medieval venue, which also houses a museum. Great works are performed by some of the finest musicians from France and around the world.

✉ 6 place Paul Painlevé ☎ 01 53 73 78 16
⊕ Fri and Sat; times vary

Odéon – Théâtre de l'Europe

Odéon, a state-funded theatre, has a long and prestigious history. In recent years, it has become a premier venue for foreign companies putting on contemporary works and student performances. France's well-known directors (such as Jean-Louis Barrault, Les Enfants du Paradis) and actors (including Madeleine Renaud) have performed here. Students of the Odéon are remembered for their scintillating performances of Beckett.

✉ 1 place Paul Claudel ☎ 01 44 41 36 36
⊕ Daily; check for times

Le Petit Journal Saint Michel

The sister venue to the Petit Journal Montparnasse, this club and restaurant in the heart of the Latin Quarter is famed for presenting some of the best jazz musicians in France, if not in the world.

✉ 71 boulevard Saint-Michel ☎ 01 43 26 28 59 ⊕ Daily from 9pm, except Sun

MARAIS AND BASTILLE

Café de la Danse

Not so much a café as a hall with auditorium seating for 300, the Café de la Danse is one of Paris' most popular venues for pop and rock concerts. Theatrical productions form part of its year-round programme, as do dance events.

✉ 5 passage Louis-Philippe ☎ 01 47 00 57 59 🕐 Daily; times vary according to the programme

Forum des Images

An inspired film theatre in the heart of the Marais district, the Forum des Images shows classics, along with clips and documentaries associated with Paris. It is a regular haunt of local residents as well as visitors to the city.

✉ porte Saint-Eustache ☎ 01 44 76 62 00 🕐 Daily; times vary according to the programme

Opéra Bastille

Perhaps the lesser known of the Paris opera houses, the Opéra Bastille nonetheless stages outstanding productions of opera, operettas, recitals and theatre, and is well frequented by locals. It is famed for having no less than five movable stages.

✉ 120 rue de Lyon ☎ 08 92 89 90 90 🕐 Daily; times vary according to the programme

Théâtre de la Bastille

New and innovative work is the focus of this theatre venue. Diehard theatre goers should check out the listings.

✉ 76 rue de la Roquette ☎ 01 43 57 42 14 🕐 Daily; times vary according to the programme

LOUVRE AND CHAMPS-ÉLYSÉES

Auditorium du Louvre

One of the most spectacular venues for musical concerts in Paris, the Auditorium du Louvre is housed underneath the Musée du Louvre's glass pyramid. With an auditorium that seats over 400, it hosts events most lunchtimes and evenings.

✉ Musée du Louvre ☎ 01 40 20 55 55

🕐 Daily; times vary according to the programme

Barramundi

Influences from India and Africa combine to give this lounge club, bar and restaurant a distinctive atmosphere. Its music and menu take their inspiration from countries and continents around the world.

✉ 3 rue Taitbout ☎ 01 47 70 21 21 🕐 Daily noon to 3pm, Sat evening 7–2am; closed Sun

Comédie Française/Salle Richelieu

Founded in the 17th century by Molière, the Comédie Française is a Parisian institution. France's best-loved actors form its troupe, and perform everything from Molière to Shakespeare and contemporary theatrical works.

✉ 1 place Colette ☎ 01 44 58 14 00 🕐 Daily; times vary according to the programme

MONTMARTRE

Bouffes du Nord

The well-known director Peter Brook's name is synonymous with this venue, which was a dying institution when he took it over. Think of the epic 8-hour long *Mahabharata*, performed in 1985 with a dazzling international cast, think of *The Death of Krishna* (2004) and other notable performances. These were ground-breaking works and set the tone for innovative productions for which the theatre has since made a name.

✉ 37 bis boulevard de la Chapelle ☎ 01 46 07 34 50 🕐 Daily, except Sun; times vary according to the programme

Divan du Monde and Divan Japonais

Housed in a former brothel, the Divan du Monde and the Divan Japonais host concerts of musical genres from rock to indy. Visitors have a choice of two floors, usually crowded, to let down their hair and dance away the evenings.

⊠ 75 rue des Martyrs ☎ 01 42 52 02 46
🕒 Daily; times vary according to programme

Olympic Café

For music from around the world and a real bohemian atmosphere, you will love this café-restaurant. Six nights a week you can enjoy various kinds of music in the basement: fusion, French *chanson*, Portuguese soul music, African rock, gypsy songs, Indian classical and even true jazz and blues.

⊠ 20 rue Léon 🕒 Tue–Sun 11am–2am

Moulin Rouge

Famed the world over for its bright red windmill outside and the raunchy stage shows inside, the Moulin Rouge, which dates from 1889, is a must on a visit to Paris. Made famous by the artist Toulouse Lautrec, whose paintings hang in the Musée d'Orsay, it was where the risqué can-can dance was first performed.

⊠ 82 boulevard de Clichy ☎ 01 53 09 82 82
🕒 Daily from 7pm

Studio 28

This is the place to go in Paris to see the newest film releases that literally change every few days. Studio 28 is a chic, modernist building in the heart of Montmartre. A bar and garden provide the perfect place to relax before or after a showing.

⊠ 10 rue Tholozé ☎ 01 46 06 36 07
🕒 Daily; times vary

FURTHER AFIELD

Centre National de la Danse

The national dance centre has 11 bright and airy studios in an old building converted with hi-tech architectural élan to suit the purpose. Dance and theatre lovers can spend an entire day at workshops, training sessions and exhibitions. There is also a large archive resource and library.

⊠ 1 rue Victor Hugo ☎ 01 41 83 27 27
🕒 Daily; check for times

Cartoucherie

Several theatre companies operate from here, so you have a wide choice of what to see.
Théâtre du Soleil (tel: 01 43 74 24 08)
Théâtre de l'Épée de Bois (tel: 01 48 08 39 74)
Théâtre de la Tempête (tel: 01 43 28 36 36)
Théâtre du Chaudron (tel: 01 43 28 97 04)
Théâtre de l'Aquarium (tel: 01 43 74 99 61)

⊠ route du Champ de Manoeuvre

Théâtre National de Chaillot

Look out for what's on in this theatre while you are in town as there is always something new and exciting, and you might even recognise a well-known actor's face among the audience.

⊠ Palais de Chaillot, 1 place du Trocadéro
☎ 01 53 65 30 00 🕒 Daily; times vary according to programme

Regard du Cygne

Here's your chance to step into the spotlight – you can perform impromptu (or prepared) for 10 minutes before an eager audience in this avant-garde theatre, where an expectant audience gathers to check out exciting new talent

⊠ 210 rue de Belleville ☎ 01 43 58 55 93
🕒 Daily; times vary according to programme

Travel Facts

Monuments and museums may take up most of your time during a sightseeing visit to Paris, so be forewarned of a few essentials. Remember that Parisians love their lunch break between 1pm and 3pm and some museums may be closed at this time. It's best to check first with the Office du Tourisme et des Congrès de Paris (www.parisinfo. com). The *Paris Carte-Musées-Monuments*, a *carnet* (travel pass) and a city map are wise investments. Forward plannning is, of course, the most sensible way to maximise on the limited time you have and also to make best use of your budget.

ARRIVING

Entry formalities

Citizens of EU countries, the USA, Canada, Australia and New Zealand do not need a visa to enter France, and therefore Paris, if staying for less than three months, but it is advisable to always carry a valid passport with at least three months left before its expiry. Citizens from countries outside of these countries should consult their respective embassies to check current formalities prior to travelling.

Airports

Paris is served by two airports, the Roissy Charles de Gaulle airport (tel: 01 48 62 22 80; www.adp/fr), where most international flights arrive, and Orly airport (tel: 01 49 75 15 15 www.adp.fr), which tends to cater for domestic flights with the occasional flight from elsewhere.

Airport Transfers

Réseau Express Régional (RER) train services run every 15 minutes from Roissy Charles de Gaulle for the 35-minute journey into the city centre. Taxis, which cost around €50 (but should be confirmed before travelling), can be found at the taxi rank outside the airport's three terminals.

Orly is a much smaller airport, located around 14km south of the city centre. It is served by Air France which provides shuttle buses to Les Invalides and Gare Montparnasse every 15 minutes or so. To travel into the city centre by train, take the Orlyval train two stops to Antony and change for the RER service into Paris. Taxis, which cost around €35 (but confirm before travelling), can be found in the taxi rank outside the airport. All journeys will take around 30 minutes.

Across the Channel

The Channel Tunnel connecting Britain and France is operated by Eurotunnel. It is one of the most popular ways to come into the country as you can take your car across in a shuttle train which, on the Dover–Calais route takes about 30 minutes. Once on it, you can leave your car and stretch your legs on the train. There are also ferries, which take about 60–90 minutes on the shorter crossings. Longer westward routes can take up to six hours, although fast ferries cut this by about half.

By Bus

Both airports have good bus connections to the city centre. Roissy Charles de Gaulle (bus terminal), which is located around 23km northwest of Paris, for instance, has Air France operating bus services (www.cars-airfrance.com) every 30 minutes to Montparnasse and Gare de Lyon, and every 15 minutes to the Arc de Triomphe and Porte Maillot. There is also the Roissybus that runs every 15 minutes to the Opéra.

By Train

There are five major international railway stations in Paris, operated by the SNCF (state railway system). The main station is the Gare de Lyon in eastern Paris, the others being Gare de l'Est, Gare du Nord, Gare St-Lazare and Gare Montparnasse. All are served by the Métro, bus and RER trains.

If travelling from the UK, the Eurostar (tel: 08705 186 186; www.eurostar.com) is the fastest way to arrive by train, and stops in the heart of Paris at the Gare du Nord station. Both the Métro and RER train services provide onward journeys throughout the city. The journey time is around 2 hours 45 minutes.

CLIMATE

One of the most popular times to visit Paris is in the springtime when temperatures can reach around 15.5°C (60°F) with a good number of sunshine hours, although from around June onwards through to August the days are much sunnier and warmer.

Autumn brings with it crisper days, but these are ideal for wrapping yourself up warmly and getting out and about. Winter temperatures rarely go below freezing, but the city can turn a magical white as snow falls from time to time. January through to March is characterised by rain.

DRIVING

Paris is a fast and frenetic city, and drivers unfamiliar with its layout may find themselves struggling. The city is circled by the Boulevard Périphérique, a multi-lane outer ring road with exits (*portes*) to parts of Paris along its route. Always be sure which *porte* you will need and get into the right lane as soon as is appropriate. Signposts are plentiful, although less so when driving around the suburbs.

When parking it is best to use public car parks as even though cars may be parked along the roadside they may be illegally parked. Fines for illegal parking are hefty. Always ensure your car is locked, even when using a public car park, and that no valuables are left inside.

There are numerous car rental companies where you can hire a vehicle providing you meet their terms and conditions. The big companies have counters at the airport and offices at various sites in the city. Avis (www.avis.com) gives good weekend rates.

The driver of the party will need to have a full driving licence. An international licence is unlikely to be required, but in the case of a UK licence the company will probably expect to see both the pink photo card and the separate green part. The driver will need to be 18 years or over, and some companies will even insist on a minimum age of 21. It is wise to check the terms and conditions thoroughly when making a booking prior to travelling and therefore avoid any problems when attempting to collect a vehicle.

ELECTRICITY

The voltage in France is 220v with two round pin sockets, so to use a UK three-prong plug you will need an adapter.

EMBASSIES AND CONSULATES
Australia: 4 rue Jean-Rey
Tel: 01 40 59 33 00
Canada: 35 avenue Montaigne
Tel: 01 44 43 29 00

Canadian Consulate: 35 avenue Montaigne
Tel: 01 44 43 29 00
New Zealand: 7 rue Léonard de Vinci
Tel: 01 45 01 43 43
South Africa: 59 quai d'Orsay
Tel: 01 53 59 23 23
UK: 35 rue du Faubourg-Saint-Honoré
Tel: 01 44 51 31 00
UK Consulate: 15 rue d'Anjou
Tel: 01 44 51 31 01/2
USA: 2 avenue Gabriel
Tel: 01 43 12 22 22

EMERGENCY TELEPHONE NUMBERS

Emergency: 112
Ambulance: 15
Fire service: 18
Police: 17
Anti poison advice: 01 40 05 48 48
Car breakdown: 01 47 07 99 99
SOS Doctor: 01 43 77 77 77;
01 47 77 77 77
Crisis line in English: 01 46 21 46 46,
available 3pm–11pm daily.

GETTING AROUND

Métro and RER

The Métro, which is largely underground, and the RER, which provides train services to and from the suburbs, are two interconnected systems that are fast, inexpensive and efficient. To use the Métro system, simply look at the station at the end of the line on the map and check the line number. These two pieces of information will appear on the front of the train. Métro stops, of which there are more than 300, are clearly identified on all Paris city maps.

Trains run from 5:30am in the morning through to 12:30am, and you will need a ticket for your journey which must be kept in order to pass through the barriers at the exit station. Combined tickets for use on the Métro and RER systems in the city centre, along with buses, are available to purchase singularly or in a book of 10 known as a *carnet*. Prices are defined by the length of the journey and the zones which you would pass through, but buying a *carnet* is the cheapest option.

HEALTH AND INSURANCE

The Paris medical system is one of the best in the world. In the event of an emergency, the city's hospitals have 24-hour care available as well as specialist doctors. For minor problems, call in at a pharmacy. These can be identified by an illuminated green cross outside their premises. Pharmacies are usually open from 9am to 7pm, Monday to Saturday, with a rota system in place for cover outside these times. A 24-hour pharmacy is at 84 avenue des Champs-Élysées (tel: 01 45 62 02 41).

The cost of treatment in Paris can be expensive, so be sure to have adequate medical insurance. Citizens of the European Union are entitled to emergency medical treatment and should be sure to take a European Health Insurance Card (EHIC) with them. Visitors from countries outside the EU should have private medical insurance in place.

LANGUAGE

Knowing even a few basic words and phrases in the local language is always a great advantage in any city, and the French particularly love a visitor who can communicate with them in French.

Basic words and phrases

Yes	oui
No	non
Please	s'il vous plaît
Thank you	merci
Excuse me	excusez-moi
I am sorry	pardon
Good morning	bonjour
Good evening	bonsoir
Good night	bonne nuit
Goodbye	au revoir

I have ...	j'ai
It is	c'est
Do you speak English	Parlez-vous anglais?
I do not understand	je ne comprends pas
When	quand
Yesterday	hier
Today	aujourd'hui
Tomorrow	demain
At what time...?	À quelle heure...?
Where is ...?	Où est...?
Here	Ici
There	là
Near	près
Before	avant
In front of	devant
Behind	derrière
Opposite	en face de
Right	à droite
Left	à gauche
Straight on	tout droit
Car park	un parking
Petrol station	un poste à essence
Parking	stationnement
Prohibited	interdit
Bridge	le pont
street	la rue
Bus stop	l'arrêt du bus
Underground station	la station de Métro
Railway station	la gare
Platform	le quai

Numbers and quantity

One	un
Two	deux
Three	trois
Four	quatre
Five	cinq
Six	six
Seven	sept
Eight	huit
Nine	neuf
Ten	dix
A little	un peu
Much/many	beacoup
Too much/many	trop

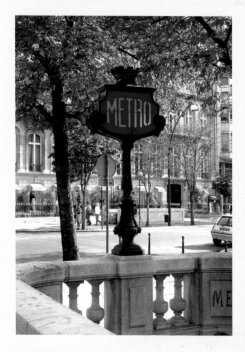

LOST PROPERTY

Any property left in public areas should be taken to the police lost property office at 36 rue des Morillons 75015 (tel: 08 21 00 25 25). If property is lost in the suburbs it is likely to be taken to the nearest police station. The procedure for reclaiming your property is simple and straightforward, and most police officers will have a good command of English. Reporting a theft or some lost property should be done at a police station, and a copy of all of the relevant paperwork retained for personal and insurance purposes.

MONEY MATTERS

All over the city there are bureaux de change, so changing money is no problem. However, the exchange rate and commission fees vary from place to place. The best bet is to go to the bank where a fee of 1–2 per cent is normal for travellers' cheques, and 2–4 per cent on cash. Be a little wary of exchange bureaux; the ones on the Champs Élysées are the most reliable. For the latest rate, consult the Currency Converter website www.oanda.com.

The major credit and debit cards are widely accepted, except perhaps in some smaller hotels and shops. Withdrawing money using a debit card can be expensive as up to 5 per cent can be charged on the amount and there is usually a minimum charge. Credit cards can be used for withdrawing money at banks provided you have proof of identity.

Banking hours are Monday to Friday 9am to 4pm or 5pm. Bureaux de change stay open longer, till 7pm in town, 10pm at railway stations and 11pm at airports.

NATIONAL HOLIDAYS

On these days, banks, post offices and other administrative offices and some monuments and museums are closed. Almost everything is closed on 1 May.

1 January: New Year's Day
Easter, variable: Sunday and Monday
2nd Monday after Easter: Whit Monday
6th Thursday after Easter: Ascension Day
1 May: May Day
8 May: Victory Day (1945)
14 July: Bastille Day
15 August: Assumption Day
1 November: All Saints' Day
11 November: Armistice Day
25 December: Christmas Day

OPENING HOURS

Business establishments are open Monday to Saturday from 8pm or 9am to 6:30pm–7:30pm. Food shops normally stay open all week until Sunday afternoon. Restaurants, bars and cafés are often closed on Sunday or Monday, and some even on Saturday. Most close around 10pm while bars and cafés may stay open until 2am. Museums open between 9am and 10am and close

around 5pm or 6pm. During summer (mid-May to mid-September) some may stay open longer. They are usually closed Monday or Tuesday, so check beforehand.

POSTAL SERVICES

The main office is at 52 rue du Louvre, open 24 hours for all postal services. Other post offices (*bureaux de poste* or PTT) open Monday to Friday 8am–7pm, Saturday 8am–noon. The address for *poste restante* mail is: Poste Restante, 52 rue du Louvre, 75001 Paris RP, France. Stamps are also available from tobacconists' shops (*tabacs*).

SECURITY

In recent years there have been several unpleasant incidents of racial harassment, although by and large Parisians are cosmopolitan in outlook and tourists are a part of life. You should carry your passport at all times as it is a legal requirement to have some form of identification on you.

TELEPHONE NUMBERS/CODES

French phone numbers comprise 10 digits and all numbers for Paris begin with 01. There are no area codes. Dial 13 for the operator and 12 for directory enquiries. For international calls, dial 00 before the country code. For international directory enquiries, dial 32 12 and the country code.
Australia 61
New Zealand 64
UK 44
US and Canada 1

TOURIST OFFICES

The main office is the Office du Tourisme et des Congrès de Paris (tel: 01 92 68 30 00), which has several branch offices at all the railway stations and at the Tour Eiffel. Another useful source of information is located at the Hôtel de Ville information office (tel: 01 42 76 43 43).

Index

A
accommodation 162-165
airports and airport transfers 184
Allée de l'Observatoire 56
antiques 173, 176
Arab World Institute 54-55
Arc de Triomphe 9, 102-105
Arènes de Lutèce 44
Army Museum 22
art nouveau architecture 134
auction house 108
avenue des Champs-Élysées 8, 101, 106-107
Axe Historique 105, 148

B
banks 188
Bastille see Marais and Bastille
Bastille Day 104, 107
Beaubourg Centre see Centre Georges Pompidou
Bibliothèque Nationale de France-François Mitterrand 44
Bibliothèque Publique d'Information 84
boat trips 72-73
Bois de Boulogne 142
Boulangerie Poilâne 68
bridges
  Passerelle Solférino 29, 73
  Pont Alexandre III 17, 30-31, 72-73
  Pont de l'Alma 32, 72
  Pont des Arts 73, 124
  Pont de Bir-Hakeim 33
  Pont du Carrousel 73
  Pont de la Concorde 73, 123
  Pont Marie 66
  Pont Neuf 43, 67, 73
  Pont Royal 73, 125
bureaux de change 188
buses 184
business hours 188

C
Café Beaubourg 80
Café de Flore 45
car rental 185
Carnavalet Museum 88
Centre d'Art Contemporain 23
Centre Georges Pompidou 9, 78, 81-84
Centre of Industrial Design 84
Centre National de la Danse 181
Champ de Mars 16, 18
Champs-Élysées 8, 101, 106-107

Channel Tunnel 184
Chantilly 9, 143
Château de Versailles see Versailles
churches
  Église Saint-Étienne-du-Mont 49
  Église Saint-Eustache 85
  Église Saint-Germain-des-Prés 8-9, 50
  Église St-Jean-de-Montmartre 130, 134
  Église Saint-Louis 53
  Église Saint-Merri 86
  Église Saint-Séverin 51
  Église Saint-Sulpice 52
  Notre-Dame 8, 42, 62-65
  Sacré-Coeur 9, 130, 136-139
  Sainte-Chapelle 70-71
Cimetière de Montmartre 130, 132
cinema 178, 179, 180, 181
Cité de la Musique 154
Cité de Sciences 154
climate and seasons 184-185
Cognacq-Jay Museum 89
Collège de France 74
Comédie Française 180
Conciergerie 42, 46-47
Conseil Constitutionnel 110
Conservatoire National des Arts et Métiers 91
credit and debit cards 188

D
Les Deux Magots 48
Diana, Princess of Wales 32
Disneyland Resort Paris 144-145
driving 185
Drouot Richelieu 108

E
École Militaire 16, 18
Église Saint-Étienne-du-Mont 49
Église Saint-Eustache 85
Église Saint-Germain-des-Prés 8-9, 50
Église St-Jean-de-Montmartre 130, 134
Église Saint-Louis 53
Église Saint-Merri 86
Église Saint-Séverin 51
Église Saint-Sulpice 52
Eiffel Tower 9, 16, 34-38
electricity 185
embassies and consulates 185-186
emergency telephone numbers 186
entertainment 178-181
Espace Dalí 135
Eugène Delacroix National Museum 69
Explor@dome 142

F
fashion 9, 127
Fête de la Musique 9
flea market 149
Fontainebleau 146-147
foreign exchange 187-188
Forest of Fontainebleau 146, 147

G
Galérie des Glaces 159
Galerie Nationale du Jeu de Paume 111
Galeries Lafayette 126
Galeries Vivienne and Colbert 109
Georges Pompidou Centre 9, 78, 81-84
Grand Palais 73, 106, 121
Grand Trianon 159
La Grande Arche 9, 148
Grande Galerie de l'Évolution 61
Gustave Moreau Museum 112

H
Hall of Mirrors 159
Hébert Museum 68
horse racing 142
Hôtel Amelot de Bisseuil 97
Hôtel de Crillon 122
Hôtel des Invalides see Les Invalides
Hôtel Hénault de Cantobre 87
Hôtel Salé 93
Hôtel de Vibraye 97

I
Île de la Cité 46, 73, 75, 124
Île Saint-Louis 53, 73
Institut de France 124
Institut du Monde Arabe 54-55
Institut National de l'Histoire de l'Art 109
insurance 186
Les Invalides 9, 17, 19-22
Islands of the Swans 33

J
Jardin d'Acclimatation 142
Jardin du Luxembourg 8, 43, 56-57
Jardin du Palais-Royal 110
Jardin des Plantes 61
Jardin des Tuileries 8, 100, 111
Jardins du Trocadèro 16, 28
Jewish History and Art, Museum of 90
Jewish quarter 96

Acknowledgements

The Automobile Association would like to thank the following photographers, companies and picture libraries for their assistance in the preparation of this book.

Abbreviations for the picture credits are as follows – (t) top; (b) bottom; (c) centre; (l) left; (r) right; (AA) AA World Travel Library.

F/C (a) Chateau de Versailles; AA/D Noble; (b) Pompidou Centre, AA/W Voysey; (c) Eiffel Tower, AA/T Souter; (d) La Grande Arche, AA/J Tims; (e) Pompidou Centre, AA/C Sawyer; (f) Arc de Triomphe, AA/M Jourdan; (g) Place de la Bastille, AA/P Kenward; (h) Jardin de Tulieres, AA/C Sawyer; (i) Sacre Coeur, AA/T Souter; (j) Notre Dame, AA/T Souter; (k) Pont-Neuf, AA/T Souter; 3 AA/T Souter; 4l AA/C Sawyer; 4c AA/M Jourdan; 4r AA/C Sawyer; 5l AA/P Kenward; 5c AA/T Souter; 5r AA/M Jourdan; 6/7 AA/M Jourdan; 8/9 AA/T Souter; 12t AA/B Rieger; 12bl AA/M Jourdan;12c AA/C Sawyer; 12br AA/C Sawyer; 13t AA/C Sawyer; 13b AA/P Enticknap; 14 AA/B Rieger;15 AA/P Enticknap; 16t AA/T Souter; 16b AA/P Kenward; 16r AA/M Jourdan; 17l AA/M Jourdan; 17r AA/M Jourdan;18 AA/M Jourdan; 19 AA/K Paterson; 20 AA/K Paterson; 21t AA/K Paterson; 21b AA/M Jourdan; 22 AA/J Tims; 23 AA/M Jourdan; 24 AA/P Enticknap; 25 AA/J Tims; 26 AA/B Rieger; 27 AA/M Jourdan; 28 AA/T Souter; 29 © BRIAN HARRIS/Alamy; 30/1 AA/B Rieger; 31 AA/M Jourdan; 32 AA/T Souter; 33 AA/M Jourdan; 34/5 AA/C Sawyer; 36 AA/K Paterson; 37t AA/P Kenward; 37b AA/J Tims; 38 AA/M Jourdan; 39 AA/C Sawyer; 40 AA/C Sawyer; 41 AA/T Souter; 42t AA/M Jourdan; 42b AA/C Sawyer; 42r AA/K Paterson; 43l AA/T Souter; 43r AA/B Rieger; 44t AA/M Jourdan; 44b © Pictures Colour Library/David Barnes; 45 AA/B Rieger; 46/7 AA/T Souter; 47 AA/M Jourdan; 48 AA/K Paterson; 49 AA/K Paterson; 50 AA/K Paterson; 51 AA/C Sawyer; 52 AA/M Jourdan; 53 AA/C Sawyer; 54/5 AA/C Sawyer; 55 AA/M Jourdan; 56/7 AA/T Souter; 58 AA/C Sawyer; 59 AA/P Kenward; 60 AA/K Paterson; 61 AA/J Tims; 62/3 AA/C Sawyer; 63 AA/C Sawyer; 64 AA/C Sawyer; 65t AA/C Sawyer; 65b AA/C Sawyer; 66 © David L. Moore/Alamy; 67 AA/B Rieger; 68 AA/C Sawyer; 69 © Directphoto.org/Alamy; 70/71 AA/K Paterson; 71 AA/J Tims; 72 AA/T Souter; 72/3 AA/M Jourdan; 74 AA/M Jourdan; 75 © Arco Images/Alamy; 76 AA/C Sawyer; 77 AA/J Tims; 78tl AA/M Jourdan; 78tr AA/C Sawyer; 78cl AA/M Jourdan; 78cr AA/M Jourdan; 78b AA/P Kenward; 80 AA/B Rieger; 81 AA/W Voysey; 82/3 AA/M Jourdan; 83 AA/M Jourdan; 84t AA/C Sawyer; 84b AA/M Jourdan; 85 AA/J Tims; 86 © guichaoua/Alamy; 87 AA/C Sawyer; 88 AA/M Jourdan; 89 © PjrFoto.com/Phil Robinson/Alamy; 90 AA/M Jourdan; 91 AA/P Kenward; 92 AA/M Jourdan; 93 AA/P Kenward; 94 ©Stefano Bianchetti/CORBIS; 95 AA/M Jourdan; 96 AA/C Sawyer; 97 AA/C Sawyer; 98 AA/M Jourdan; 99 AA/C Sawyer; 100t AA/M Jourdan;100b AA/C Sawyer; 100r AA/M Jourdan; 101l AA/M Jourdan; 101r AA/M Jourdan; 102 AA/P Enticknap; 103 AA/J Tims; 104 AA/K Paterson; 105t AA/M Jourdan; 105b AA/M Jourdan; 106 AA/M Jourdan; 107a AA/C Sawyer; 107b AA/M Jourdan; 108 © SCHIFRES LUCAS/CORBIS SYGMA;109 AA/M Jourdan; 110 AA/M Jourdan; 111 AA/C Sawyer; 112 AA/J Tims; 113 AA/P Kenward;114 AA/M Jourdan;115 AA/M Jourdan; 116/17t AA/J Tims; 116/17b AA/J Tims; 117 AA/M Jourdan; 118/19 AA/K Paterson; 119 AA/M Jourdan; 120 AA/K Paterson; 121 AA/K Paterson; 122/3 AA/M Jourdan; 123 AA/M Jourdan; 124 AA/M Jourdan; 125 © David A. Barnes/Alamy; 126 AA/K Paterson; 127 AA/C Sawyer; 128t AA/T Souter; 128b AA/K Paterson; 129 AA/B Rieger; 130tl AA/P Kenward; 130tr AA/C Sawyer; 130cl AA/C Sawyer; 130cr AA/M Jourdan; 130b © Dennis Smith/Imagesfrance.com/ Alamy;132 AA/P Kenward;133 © Dennis Smith/Imagesfrance.com/Alamy;134 AA/C Sawyer;135 AA/C Sawyer; 136/7 AA/K Paterson; 137 AA/M Jourdan; 138 AA/J Tims; 139 AA/C Sawyer; 140t AA/M Jourdan;140b AA/K Paterson; 141 AA/T Souter; 142 AA/K Paterson; 143 AA/D Noble; 144/5 © Disney; 145 © Disney;146/7 AA/D Noble;147 AA/M Jourdan; 148 AA/J Tims; 149 AA/C Sawyer; 150 AA/J Tims; 151 AA/J Tims; 152 © The Garden Picture Library/Alamy; 153 © guichaoua/Alamy; 154 AA/J Tims; 155 AA/M Jourdan; 156/7 AA/D Noble; 157 AA/M Jourdan; 158 AA/M Jourdan; 159 AA/M Jourdan; 160t AA/M Jourdan; 160b AA/B Rieger; 161 AA/C Sawyer; 162 AA/C Sawyer; 166 AA/C Sawyer; 172 AA/C Sawyer; 178 AA; 182 AA/M Jourdan;183 AA/ C Sawyer; 185 AA; 187 AA/T Souter.

Every effort has been made to trace the copyright holders, and we apologise in advance for any accidental errors. We would be happy to apply the corrections in the following edition of this publication.

The Automobile Association would like to thank all other contributors to this publication.